THE MASTER ARCHITECT SERIES IV

Richard Dattner

Selected and Current Works of
Richard Dattner & Partners Architects

First published in Australia in 2000 by
The Images Publishing Group Pty Ltd
ACN 059 734 431
6 Bastow Place, Mulgrave, Victoria, 3170
Telephone (61 3) 9561 5544 Facsimile (61 3) 9561 4860

National Library of Australia Cataloguing-in-Publication Data

      Richard Dattner & Partners Architects.
      Richard Dattner : selected and current works
      of Richard Dattner & Partners Architects.

      Includes index.
      ISBN 1 86470 053 X.
      ISSN 1320 7253

      1. Richard Dattner & Partners Architects. 2. Architecture,
      Modern—20th century—United States. 3. Architects—
      United States. 4. Architecture, American. I. Dattner,
      Richard, 1948–. II. Title.(Series: Master architect series IV).

720.973

Edited by Renée Otmar, Otmar Miller Consultancy Pty Ltd
Designed by The Graphic Image Studio Pty Ltd,
Mulgrave, Australia
Printed in Hong Kong

Dedication

This book is dedicated to all those whose efforts are essential in the realization of our work:

the private and public clients who entrust us with their aspirations;

the members of our staff whose contributions are here made tangible;

the consultants who help resolve the many technical challenges;

the public servants who review and monitor design and construction;

the men and women who build and manage what we design; and

the many thousands who daily use the results of this miraculous collaboration.

We thank you all.

Richard Dattner & Partners Architects

Contents

Preface

Assembling this monograph has granted me the unique opportunity to step back from the concerns of individual projects in order to gain some sense of the direction our architectural practice has taken since it was founded. The project opposite—a recent proposal for a circular pedestrian overpass creating a focal point for the intersection of nine traffic routes at Lincoln Center—illustrates several recurrent themes in our work:

Celebration of the Quotidian: *recognizing the heroic quality of everyday life—in structures that attempt to ennoble "ordinary" existence.*

Place-making: *creating a memorable place, so when you get there, "there is a there, there".*

Respect for Context: *achieving a balance between a building and its context, where both can have their voice heard—with neither drowning out the other.*

Economy of Means: *conserving the material, human, and natural resources of our finite planet—and of those who fund these projects.*

Concern for the User: *to "first, do no harm", and also to improve local conditions with each project.*

Attention to Materials and Structure: *celebrating the struggle against gravity, and limiting the ravages of time on what we build.*

An Attempt at Connection: *knitting together the complex strands of the urban fabric.*

The process of designing and realizing the projects that follow in these pages has been, and continues to be, one of significant challenge, intriguing variety, and intense personal gratification. Many individuals have helped in their realization, and I thank them here again.

I am grateful also to this country in which I made my home, and for this city in which I found everything I had ever hoped for in architecture—like-minded colleagues, responsive clients, and an endlessly fascinating community to use and enjoy the fruits of our continuing collaboration.

Richard Dattner, FAIA

New York City, 2000

1

1 Circular pedestrian overpass suspended over difficult intersection
2 A floating ring connects sidewalks, and bridges roadways
Following pages:
New York Ferry Terminal proposal

2

"Any architect willing to endure the often brutal process of working for a government agency deserves a purple heart.

"An architect like Richard Dattner, who has been through the process repeatedly and nonetheless sustained a level of quality as high as that shown by his designs for Riverbank State Park, sewage treatment plants and public school buildings, should be given a ticker tape parade up Broadway."

Herbert Muschamp
The New York Times, April 14, 1996

Introduction

Richard Dattner Architect

by Jayne Merkel

Civil Architect

As architecture reflects the tenor of the times, so too are architects products of their own unique circumstances. Richard Dattner's were unusual—and formative. "My concern with the civility, order, and accessibility of a shared public environment had its genesis in the incivility, chaos, and terror of the wartime Poland my parents and I fled in 1940," he explains. The family traveled first to Italy, then to Cuba, and finally to the United States, before Dattner was nine years old. "I was especially sensitive to each of these new cultures," he writes, "and as each new language was superimposed on those preceding, the non-verbal syntax of form, light, and place became for me the constant language with which I am still most at home." Although architecture became Dattner's "constant language," his fluency in Spanish later helped him work with neighborhood groups in bilingual communities such as New York's Washington Heights, where he now lives. Most American architects work either only at the local level, or only at the international level. Dattner has worked outside New York, but remains first and foremost a local architect, rooted in the communities of his chosen hometown.

The wanderings of Dattner's early childhood, which created a desire for stability and roots, ended when his family moved from Cuba to Jackson Heights, Queens, and finally to Buffalo—all in 1946. Buffalo, with its gargantuan steel mills, grain elevators, Louis Sullivan's Guaranty Building, and Frank Lloyd Wright's Darwin Martin House, remained the Dattner family home, where the architect lived until he enrolled at the Massachusetts Institute of Technology in 1955. The public high schools he attended in Buffalo (one, an imposing Victorian edifice and the other, a modest-but-stately Georgian block) are inscribed on his memory, and served as benchmarks for the schools and modular prototypes he later designed for the New York City School Construction Authority.

At MIT, Dattner was impressed both by the monumentality and surprising internal flexibility of Welles Bosworth's self-assured stone classicism, and by the humane, modern brick dormitory by Alvar Aalto. Echoes of the undulating façade of Aalto's Baker House are found in the sweeping curves that reappear in his work. Lewis Mumford, who "illuminated the link between architecture and the culture in which it is created," and Joseph Hudnut, whose "illustrated lectures on architectural history taught, as a subtext, the primacy of substance over style," were significant figures for Dattner at MIT.

Dattner attended London's Architectural Association in 1957–58. It was, he says, "a pivotal moment, when the British New Brutalists—James Stirling, James Gowan, and Peter and Alison Smithson—were looking for a direction for modern architecture that would express the striving for social justice, the limited resources available, and the growing complexity of post-war urban life." After college Dattner moved to New York, because it seemed to be a meritocracy filled with opportunity. And so it was—he has embraced those opportunities, and continues to pursue them with steadfast optimism.

1

1   MIT Central Athletic Facility proposal

Against the Tide

Richard Dattner has spent most of his career swimming upstream, against the tide of architectural fashion. When he opened his practice in New York City in the 1960s, he designed playgrounds, housing projects, and some light industrial buildings. When federal funding began to dry up and most architects abandoned the public sector, his firm remained committed to public work. Few of those who continued to specialize in building public facilities pursued them with the same ambition; hardly any have tackled projects on such a wide variety of scales, of so many building types. And though many architects repeated the modernist mantra throughout the postmodern era, few really allowed function to define form, or remained primarily committed to social programs.

An apt metaphor for Dattner's practice may be the swimming pool he designed for the 1998 Goodwill Games on Long Island. It had to be built within 18 months, accommodate 4000 people, provide handicapped access, and fit within the gentle landscape of Eisenhower Park. The friendly whale of a building ultimately realized straddles a sloping site, allowing wheelchairs access down to the pool or up to the spectator level. The structure hugs the ground and cuts into it, masking its 82,000-square foot size with a low-slung, vaulted roof and tapered concrete buttresses. Waves on its bright blue eaves, bold, earth-colored stripes on its façade, and giant elephant trunk vents help make it inviting. Tubular steel arch trusses, tall enough for competitive 10-meter diving, support skylights for natural lighting, while reducing the exposed roof surface to minimize heat loss and gain. Dattner invested the $26 million budget in features that would enable energy and maintenance costs to be saved over the long term, installing permanent seating only on the north side. For large crowds, the southern walls open to accommodate bleachers protected by fabric sunshades. As Charles Linn observed in Architectural Record, "the pool is a lot like the perfect swimmer's body—flexible, efficient, and lean, with a high strength-to-weight ratio." It isn't surprising that many competitive swimmers consider it the best pool in the country. The festive red, white and blue natatorium, which so well served the Goodwill Games, now provides Nassau County with a world-class setting for swimming and diving competitions, training, and recreational water sports.

Architecture Out of the Ordinary

Dattner's ability to make the most of scarce resources in a high-spirited way has enabled him to build schools, libraries, housing, subway stations, and parks that exceed expectations. His firm pursued the pragmatic and the here-and-now throughout the 1980s—when many in the profession valued the past more than the present, and sought meaning in symbols instead of spaces. While most other architects either joined large firms or practiced independently, Dattner put together a medium-size firm—which has grown to 40 by the time this book goes to press. Unlike firms identified with a single design approach that becomes a recognizable style, Dattner has relegated imagery to a secondary position. His work has elements which appear on several projects—curved planes, wavy canopies, patterned brick bands—but these are simple, economical means by which to humanize a building and give a place identity. The aesthetics and syntax of building forms derive from the program, site, and context. Like the architect he most respects, Renzo Piano, the process of "inventing a design language appropriate to the project" is Dattner's first step toward a design solution.

Up on the Roof

It took more than optimism to see Riverbank State Park to completion. Built to compensate the West Harlem community for having a sewage treatment plant located on its shores, the 28-acre, half-mile-long park built over the Hudson River, on the 14- section roof of the North River Pollution Treatment Facility. Riverbank was 24 years in the making, and Dattner's firm—the fourth architect to be hired—was involved for the final 15 years of the park's realization. As the architect noted in his Civil Architecture: The New Public Infrastructure (a book that is part discourse on public architecture, part autobiography; New York: McGraw-Hill, 1994), it took continuous community pressure, considerable technical expertise, constant revision, reassessment, and redesign—and $148 million. In 1993, the first year of its operation, more than 3 million visitors used its athletic fields, skating rink, swimming pools, gymnasium, stage, and other facilities. It has become, after Jones Beach, the second most visited place in the New York State Park system. And it demonstrates what a collaboration between a well-organized community, responsive government, and a concerned architect can accomplish.

"The entire park—buildings, landscaping, site features—is on a strict diet because of the limited load-bearing capacity of the plant's caissons, columns, and roof spans," Dattner explains. Visiting Riverbank feels somewhat like being on the deck of an aircraft carrier. Though born of compromise, value engineered, and designed for ease of maintenance, its red, tan, and green buildings and pavilions framing playing fields feel natural and inviting to a diverse community. Perched on the Hudson River and overlooking the Palisades and Manhattan, the fiberglass-capped roofs glow from a distance as beacons of perseverance—in a place where perseverance and hope have long been in too-short supply.

Sludge Happens

Dattner sees the full range of human experience as worthy of the architect's best efforts. Riverbank was far from his first professional encounter with sewage—he has been involved in large-scale waste treatment and sanitation projects for decades. Since, as he says, "Sludge happens," Dattner has tried to dignify a group of Sludge Dewatering Facilities which deal with this all-too-human by-product. Alternating bands of dark and light concrete panels, large window walls, and landscaping help make the facilities more attractive (if still not embraced by neighbors). His gabled Marine Transfer Stations, where barges full of solid waste leave for the Staten Island landfill and beyond, are appealing in a nautical way. The MTS at West 59th Street has a colonnaded façade crowned with a pediment, which replicates its 19-century predecessor, and a decorative rim of distinctly 20th-century neon created by the artist Steven Antonakos.

Buildings Teach

For Dattner, schools provide the best opportunities to "make the buildings which then make us," he says, quoting Winston Churchill. In 1987, New York City faced the same problems of immigration and school overcrowding it had confronted in 1887, when the Board of Education engaged one of Dattner's heroes, C.B.J. Snyder, the New York architect who built scores of handsome, imposing public school buildings, and developed the prototypical "H" plan for schools on mid-block sites. "This prototype would be repeated all over New York City, in a variety of styles," Dattner explains. One hundred years later, the newly created New York City School Construction Authority employed prototypes again—this time with four architecture firms hired to produce four different designs.

The Dattner firm was responsible for the Intermediate School prototype. Exterior treatments of these prototypes remain similar—with variations in color responding to local context—but plans are varied according to site and circumstance, by utilizing computerization and modular design. Dattner's scheme, with curves in plan and cornice, patterned brick, and accentuated square windows, come in three- and four-story versions, and accommodate 900, 1200, or 1800 students, divided into sub-schools of either 450 or 600 students. The children attend classes at the "uptown" sub-schools and go "downtown" to the central core for communal activities in the library, gym, cafeteria, and auditorium.

It Takes a Village

Dattner's most impressive schools are the ones designed specifically for their particular communities—with the families of the children who would use them actively involved. The Salomé de Henriquez Intermediate School (I.S. 218) curves around a semi-circular courtyard, across Broadway from Fort Tryon Park in upper Manhattan. It gracefully organizes classrooms and common rooms for 1800 intermediate school students into a small, irregular site, along with facilities for before-school and after-school recreational programs, and a branch of Mercy College for parents. The gated courtyard and horizontally-banded façade gives Schools Chancellor Joseph Fernandez's first "school of the future" a presence greater than its actual size might command, while relating this five-story school to mid-rise art deco apartment buildings in the neighborhood. With its clear symmetry, flat roofs, square windows, and cylindrical, central staircase banded with glass brick, it recalls both Venturi & Rauch's Guild House retirement home in Philadelphia and Susana Torre's Fire Station No. 5 in Columbus, Indiana. But the artful matter-of-factness of I.S. 218 is crowned with a meaningful flagpole, instead of the ironic antenna that Venturi used at the Philadelphia retirement home. By the side entrance to the school—where most students enter—a colorful mosaic mural by Joyce Kozloff celebrates the students' Caribbean heritage.

For a community of professionals and artists in Tribeca, Dattner participated in a true collaboration with parents, pupils, the P.S. 234 principal, elected local officials, and a neighborhood group that demanded a voice in the selection of the architect. Together, they managed to create a practical, almost magical, and whimsical building that surpasses city standards, within the budget, and in record time.

2   Tackapausha Museum, Long Island

TACKAPAUSHA
MUSEUM

2

The turreted, "L"-shaped school bends around the half-block site, turning its back on the commercial development to the south, and opening to the Washington Market Park across Chambers Street. It creates a separate precinct, its schoolyard contained by a brick arcade and wrought-iron fence designed on a nautical theme by artist Donna Dennis, who also created the ceramic medallions with scenes from old Washington Market. The building itself teaches about architectural history, with turrets on two of its four corners, segmented brick arches, and curved rooms, wall segments, and corridors. The corner bell tower (where a different student rings the school bell each morning) is also a lighthouse marking the former shoreline of lower Manhattan. The school building's decorative program is part story book and part history lesson, with references to the area's past, old New York City schools, and even Charles Rennie Mackintosh's Scotland Street School in Glasgow.

3

Shelter from the Storm

In recent years, public schools have been asked to accept responsibility for the health care, nutrition, and counseling of their students, but some children's needs are greater than any neighborhood school can meet. Richard Dattner helped the Leake & Watts Family Services in Yonkers to assist children whose extraordinary needs require a stay on a residential campus designed to provide 24-hour-a-day care in home-like, professionally-staffed "cottages". Established by the Trinity Church Parish in 1831 for children orphaned by immigration, disease, and social dislocation, it now cares for teenagers "orphaned" by drug-addicted or absent mothers and fathers. A series of environments encouraging progressively increasing personal responsibility are delineated within the nine new residential cottages, two rehabilitated cottages, and a new school. Villages of three residential cottages and a "care cottage" surround a common green. Front stoops on each cottage provide a transition between the larger community and the cottage, where 14 students and two resident counselors live; students clean their own rooms, prepare meals, and prepare for life beyond this residential community on its idyllic, Olmsted-designed campus.

In a historic McKim, Mead & White pavilion at Bellevue Hospital, the Dattner firm is now creating an Emergency Intake Center and Training Academy for New York City children in need of immediate assistance and referral to foster care. The design restores the exteriors of the 1912 R&S Building at First Avenue and 29th Street, for the New York City Administration for Children's Services, and transforms the interiors of the 117,000-square-foot Center into a training academy, offices, and child-friendly residential spaces for overnight stays.

For the needs of the other end of the life span, the firm has designed notable residential developments in Manhattan, Brooklyn, Queens, and the Bronx, for the New York Foundation for Senior Citizens. Characterized by inviting gardens and dignified interiors, these neighborhood apartment buildings provide real homes for low-income residents, within the strict budgetary limits of Federal housing standards.

3   Columbia University School of Social Work proposal
4   Columbia University 50-meter Pool and Field House

Moving Right Along

The Dattner firm is currently designing a number of transportation facilities, including New York City Transit subway stations in Queens at Queensboro Plaza, in the Bronx at Pelham Parkway, on Manhattan's West Side at Broadway and 72nd Street (with Gruzen Samton), and at 42nd Street and Eighth Avenue. For the Port Authority of New York and New Jersey, designs were implemented for passenger improvements at JFK International Airport, and a number of customer enhancements are underway at Newark International Airport.

Once in a while the firm gets the opportunity to indulge its more playful side—as do the tourists who visit the Hertz Rent-a-Car facility designed for Orlando, Florida. Bright yellow, wavy-roofed modular pavilions here protect passengers and vehicles from sun and rain, reinforce building entrances, and identify the car rental agency from the highway, while setting the tone for a fun-filled holiday at nearby Disney World. The architects and Mardan Fabricators of Fort Lauderdale—the company which manufactured the fiberglass shelters designed by Dattner— brought the Shelterscape system to market. Now available in a variety of bright colors, various widths, and numerous combinations, the modular system is used by architects throughout the United States to cover walkways, and to shelter drive-through tellers, airport terminal entrances, sidewalk cafés, and roof gardens.

An Enlightened Collaboration

In 1964, the Estée Lauder family entrusted Richard Dattner and his Cooper Union faculty colleague, Sam Brody, with the design of its first laboratory, manufacturing facility, and warehouse at the site of a former sod farm on Long Island. That building— Dattner's first major structure—won a national AIA Honor Award, and demonstrated the first large-scale application of porcelain-enamel steel panels in the United States. The Estée Lauder Company went on to become the leading cosmetics producer in the world, and in the intervening years the team of Richard Dattner–Davis Brody Bond designed facilities in the United States, Canada, Great Britain, Belgium, and Switzerland. Built over a 36-year period, these disparate projects have met CEO Leonard Lauder's consistent goal of "timeless design". The Estée Lauder projects illustrated in this monograph—corporate headquarters, research laboratories, distribution centers, and manufacturing facilities—represent a unique, long-standing collaboration between an enlightened client and his architects.

Design for Play

Recreational architecture has long been one of the firm's specialities. Richard Dattner's first public commission was for the Adventure Playground in Central Park at West 67th Street— a project funded by the Estée and Joseph Lauder Foundation, which Dattner recently redesigned with the support of Michael Bloomberg. As well as the Goodwill Games Swimming and Diving Complex, the firm has been responsible for the Asphalt Green AquaCenter on the Upper East Side of Manhattan, Riverbank State Park, Columbia University's Lawrence A. Wien Stadium, the renovation of the New York Athletic Club swimming pool

and lockers, and the Stadium at the State University of New York at Stony Brook. The architects are now at work on the David S. Pottruck Fitness Center at the University of Pennsylvania, as well as on designs for a Field House and Aquatic Facility for Columbia University. As part of New York City's bid to host the Olympic Games in 2012, the firm was commissioned to prepare designs for field hockey facilities at the Columbia University Stadium, and for a boxing venue at Harlem's historic 369th Regiment Armory.

The modestly scaled Discovery Center, at the New York Botanical Garden's Everett Children's Adventure Garden, is a learning resource within a unique landscape designed by Miceli Kulik Williams & Associates, and exhibit designers Van Sickle & Rolleri. It is a natural, magical place for wandering alone or in structured educational programs. The Discovery Center is really a gallery, classroom building, and store, but with its cedar colonnade and low-slung shingle roof, it seems almost a found object in the landscape. One of Richard Dattner's favorite slogans is the admonition from the Hippocratic oath: "First, do no harm." It is rare in architecture to aspire to such modesty, and rarer still to accomplish it. This little pavilion settles into the children's garden so gently that it is possible to visit and hardly realize that there is a building there at all.

Looking Ahead

At the beginning of this new century, Richard Dattner was joined in partnership by four of his long-time associates, and the firm was renamed Richard Dattner & Partners Architects P.C. Founding partner Richard Dattner, FAIA is joined by Joseph Coppola, AIA, William Stein, AIA, Bernard Zipprich, AIA, Beth Greenberg, AIA, and their professional colleagues, in the continuation of the firm's goal—the production of architecture "which aims at the realization of our clients' highest aspirations, respecting our shared social responsibility, and built within available resources."

Jayne Merkel edits Oculus, *the magazine of the AIA New York Chapter, and serves on the editorial board of* Architectural Design *in London. She directed the graduate program in Architecture and Design Criticism at Parsons School of Design, taught writing and art history at several other colleges, and has written for* Art in America, Artforum, Architecture, Progressive Architecture *and numerous other publications.*

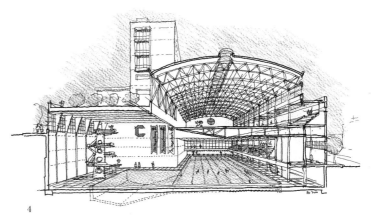

4

Learning/Play

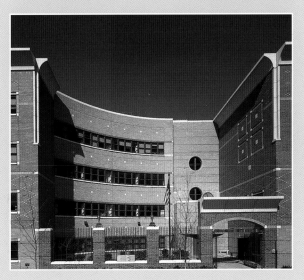

Richard Dattner & Partners Architects

Central Park Playgrounds

Design/Completion 1966/1972
New York, New York
New York City Parks & Recreation
Concrete, stone, wood, sand

Among the first of a new generation
of adventure playgrounds built in
New York City, these playgrounds
allow children freedom of movement,
experience, and challenge. A world in
miniature—mounds, streams, waterfalls,
bridges, tunnels—these play settings let
children exercise their imaginations
and learn to master increasingly
challenging environments. Sand and
water are essential components of these
playgrounds—water providing movement,
sound and color, and sand creating
a safe play surface and, mixed with water,
a construction material. Natural materials,
simple forms, and appropriate scale
allow children to safely exercise their
imaginations as well as their bodies.

The Central Park Playgrounds include
The Adventure Playground at W. 67th St;
The Ancient Play Garden at E. 85th St;
The Water Playground and Heckscher
Playground at W. 59th St; The 72nd St.
Playground on Fifth Avenue, and the
Wild West Playground at W. 91st Street.

1

1 The Ancient Play Garden on the cover of
  The New Yorker
2 Splashing pool at The Ancient Play Garden
3 Water channel at the The Water Playground

2

3

New York Botanical Garden Discovery Center

Design/Completion 1995/1998
Bronx, New York
New York Botanical Garden
Miceli Kulik Williams Landscape Architects
600 square meters
Timber structure, plank roof
Wood, asphalt shingles, tile

Funded by the Henry and Edith Everett Foundation, the Adventure Garden and Discovery Center provide New York City children with an experience of a natural ecological system, where they can learn about plants, insects, soil, and climate. Interactive exhibits, self-guided trails, explanatory graphics, and a trained staff encourage exploration, discovery, and learning.

The Discovery Center blends into its natural setting by curving gently around a restored wetland. Cedar columns, exposed timber beams, and wood plank roofing illustrate the link between nature and human-made construction. The natural landscape, building, and exhibits are designed to be experienced through all the senses.

1   Pavilion in a wetland pond
2   Elevation of Discovery Center
3   View from boardwalk, with interpretive graphics
4   First-floor plan

1

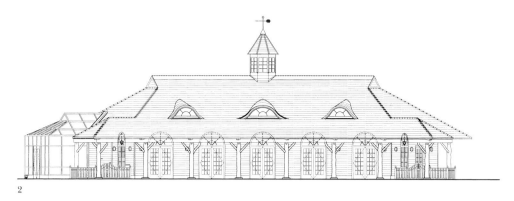

2

3

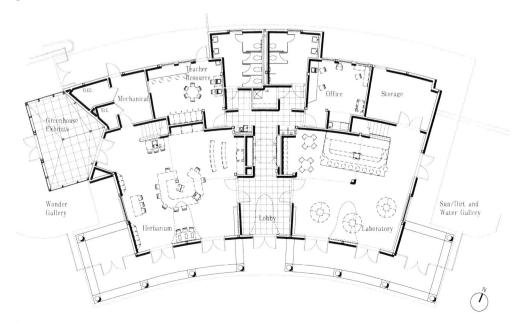

4

Primary School PS 380

Design/ Completion 1969/1980
Brooklyn, New York
New York City Board of Education
1500 pupils, 15,000 square meters
Concrete columns and slabs
Concrete, brick, structural facing tile

In order to make this 1500-student, K–4 school inviting and easy for children and parents to find their way around, a central corridor forms a "main street" from which tributary corridors serve the classrooms. This "main street" varies in width and accommodates small groups for informal learning. The organization of the three triangular classroom wings along the linear spine allows all classroom windows to face landscaped courtyards rather than the street. Nine "learning complexes" provide self-contained areas able to function as either open classrooms for team teaching or are partitioned into smaller, traditional classrooms. Ancillary spaces for each learning complex include a resource space, small rooms for individual instruction, a conference room, and storage.

The school building itself is seen as a learning experience—revealing its construction, utility systems, and operation. Ventilation ducts and electric conduits are exposed in the ceiling of the "main street", as is a glass pipe through which the drainage of rain water is visible. A picture window allows children to see the boilers, pipes, and valves in the cellar mechanical room.

1

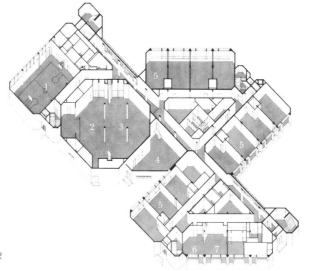

2

1 Gymnasium
2 Auditorium
3 Lunchroom
4 Kitchen
5 Learning Complex
6 Office
7 Principal

1   Stair, elevator, and boiler flue are expressed
2   Axonometric of first floor, with "main street"
3   Triangular wings shelter play spaces
4   "Main street" with mural, mirrored columns,
    and ceiling mirrors

3

4

Primary School PS 234

Design/Completion 1984/1988
New York, New York
New York City Board of Education
785 pupils, 7500 square meters
Concrete columns and slabs
Concrete, brick, structural facing tiles

Built in an historic neighborhood in lower Manhattan, the building teaches its pupils and neighborhood residents about architectural history, construction techniques, and the history of the city and its waterfront. An exterior perimeter wall echoes the surrounding 19th-century mercantile buildings, which have brick arches, curved corners, and deeply set industrial windows. The cylindrical turret is both lighthouse and castle tower—marking the former river's edge and guarding the enclosed play courtyard. Porcelain medallions and a decorative fence by artist Donna Dennis are an open book of local history, illustrating scenes from the vanished Washington Market and silhouettes of the clippers, lighters, ferries, tugboats, and barges that once sailed past this point.

Classrooms are organized around the courtyard, to maximize light and views on a site surrounded by high-rise commercial buildings. Children arrive through an entrance gate, cross the courtyard, and walk through a turret—a three-step transition from the outside world. Two smaller turrets each serve two kindergartens on the ground floor, so that the youngest children have direct access to the courtyard. Circulation spaces on each floor are widened to function as a "commons", with stepped seating where informal gatherings, performances, and study groups can take place.

1

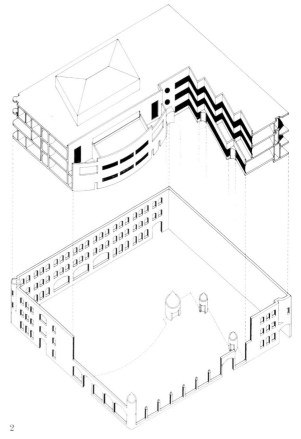

1   Entrance gate, clipper ship, and kindergarten turret
2   A modern school within a contextual perimeter enclosure
3   Lighthouse and bell tower marks original shoreline

2

4   Auditorium seats 220 persons
5   "Commons", with stepped seating and oculus
6   Kindergarten divided into activity areas
7   First-floor commons invites parents to linger

4

5

6

7

8   View from south with library corner reading
     room
9   Enclosed play courtyard creates a kid's cloister
10   Protective fence is a lesson in local history

8

9

10

Intermediate School IS 218

Design/Completion 1985/1992
New York, New York
New York City Board of Education
New York City School Construction Authority
1800 pupils, 19,000 square meters
Steel structure, concrete slabs
Steel, brick, glass block, structural facing tile

Characterized as "the school of the future" when completed, IS 218 is a real community school, where children *and* parents come to learn. Serving a predominantly Hispanic neighborhood in Washington Heights, the school houses 1800 students in the 5th through 8th grades (organized in "academies" of 600 students or less), a satellite college operated by Mercy College, and a health and after-school program run by the Children's Aid Society. The building serves community residents 15 hours a day, six days a week, year-round.

A curved façade encloses the entrance courtyard, sets classroom windows back from Broadway, and permits more classrooms to face Fort Tryon Park. A less formal side entry, enlivened by a colorful mosaic mural, serves as the main student entrance. In order to respect the unique architectural context of this neighborhood of "art-deco" apartments, the school is limited to five stories—with bands of contrasting brick, glass block, and a curved stair tower echoing features prevalent in the area. The streamlined, curved surfaces of the building, and the landscaped courtyard have proved especially popular with the Dominican community, recalling for many the buildings and gardens of their native country.

1

1 Landscaped Courtyard
2 Entrance Court
3 Staff Parking
4 Connecting Walk
5 Amphitheater
6 Running Track
7 Multi-Purpose Court
8 Play Street (School Hours)
9 Rear Yard

1 View from Fort Tryon Park
2 First-floor plan with adjoining school playground
Opposite:
   Courtyard faces across Broadway to
   Fort Tryon Park

2

0 25 50ft

4 Student entrance faces school playground
5 Auditorium seats 600 persons
6 Community entrance gate and landscaped
  courtyard
7 Gymnasium with motorized dividing wall

4

5

6

7

Maxwell High School

Design/Completion 1992/1998
Brooklyn, New York
New York City Board of Education
New York City School Construction Authority
16,000 square meters
Steel structure, concrete slabs
Brick, aluminum windows

Originally built as a prototypical elementary school in 1912, Maxwell High School underwent major rehabilitation and an expansion to double its capacity and modernize the entire facility. The new wing—one story lower in order to respect the historic original—continues the granite base, brick, and limestone string courses of the original façade, adding gently curved bays and curved roof profiles to further soften its impact.

The interior circulation of the addition extends the linear main corridor to a rotunda linking it with the central corridor of the new structure. The main entrance of the older building is preserved as the community entrance leading directly to the restored auditorium. The addition houses cafeteria and kitchen, science laboratories, mechanical spaces, and a student activity center. A large gymnasium enclosed by an arched roof occupies most of the third and fourth floors.

1

1   Pennsylvania Avenue elevation
2   New addition defers to the historic original
    building
3   First-floor plan of completed project

2

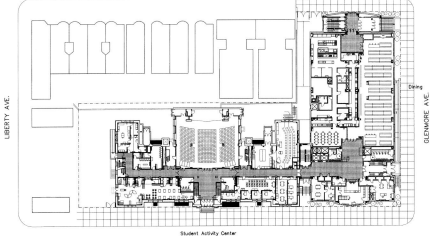

3

Prototype Intermediate Schools

Design/Completion 1988/1997
I.S. 90 Manhattan, I.S. 2 Brooklyn, I.S. 5 Queens, New York
New York City Board of Education
New York City School Construction Authority
12,600/18,900 square meters
Steel structure, concrete slabs
Patterned brick, aluminum windows, art fence

In order to reduce the time required to design, review, and build urgently needed schools, a prototypical design was developed for a series of intermediate schools serving grades 6 through 8. Assembled like *Lego* blocks, these schools combine the efficiency of a larger school with the more appropriate scale of the smaller sub-schools. The building's components can be arranged in configurations accommodating most urban sites, with variations in surface treatment relating to the character of their surrounding neighborhoods. Already completed are I.S. 90 Manhattan (1800 students), I.S. 2 Brooklyn (1200 students), and I.S. 5 Queens (1200 students). A 900-student, three-story prototype has been designed for I.S. 171 Brooklyn.

Designed as a community, the prototype has a "downtown" of shared facilities, and "uptown" neighborhoods of classrooms corresponding to the sub-schools. The "downtown" module is a four-story, rectangular structure containing administration, kitchen, and cafeteria on the first floor, library and shops on the second floor, and two-story gymnasium and auditorium spaces on the third through fourth floors. The "uptown" sub-schools serve 550 students in four-story classroom modules curved on one side to enclose landscaped courtyards—which provide separate entrances for each sub-school. Students spend most of their day in these less formal, smaller-scaled environments which are supportive of their need for individualized learning.

1

1   I.S. 90 Manhattan
2   I.S. 5 Queens
3   I.S. 2 Brooklyn, sub-school entrance

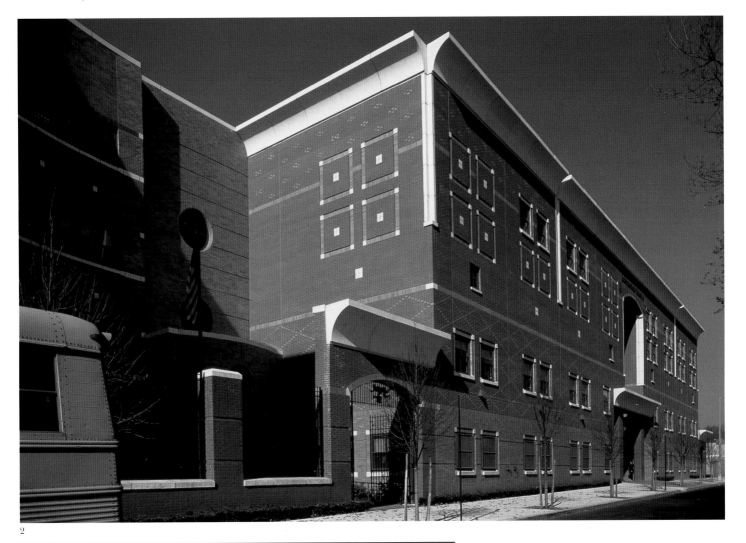

2

3

A "kit-of-parts"—four modular building sections—can be combined in several ways to fit almost any urban site. Module A contains shared auditorium, cafeteria, library, gymnasium, and administrative spaces, while modules B, C, and D comprise "sub-schools" housing classrooms. The four-story prototype houses 1200 students in two sub-schools, or 1800 students in three sub-schools. A three-story version houses 900 students in two sub-schools.

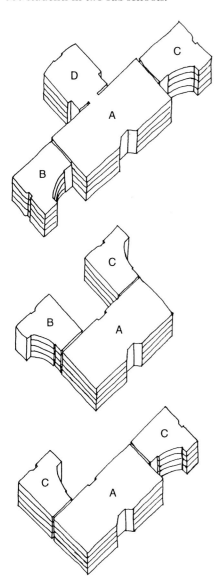

4

5

4　Axonometric of "kit-of-parts"
5　Student entrance to sub-school at I.S. 90 Manhattan
6　Sub-school entrance arch at I.S. 90 Manhattan
7　I.S. 90 ceiling mural by artist Martin Wong
8　I.S. 5 ceiling mural by artist Sung-Ho Choi
9　Wall montage by artist Sung-Ho Choi

8

6

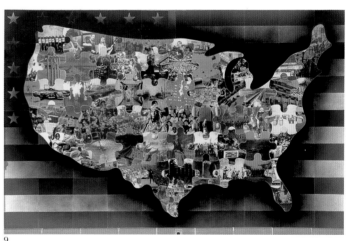

9

7

10 Divisible gymnasium at I.S. 2 Brooklyn
11 Auditorium at I.S. 2 seats 550-student
sub-school
12 Site plan of I.S. 90 Manhattan

10

11

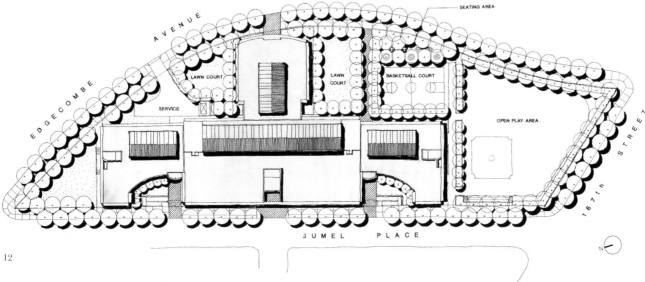

12

Primary School 15

Design/Completion 1997/1999
Yonkers, New York
Yonkers Board of Education
7500 square meters
Steel structure, concrete slabs, metal roof monitors
Brick, window walls, aluminum sun-shades

Accommodating 500 students in grades K–6, PS 15 is a community school organized like a shopping center—with the auditorium and cafeteria at one end, and the gymnasium at the opposite end anchoring a "main street" corridor lined with classrooms, library, and administration. On a sloping site, the uphill, two-story façade is similar in scale to surrounding single-family homes, and is divided into classroom-width bays topped with curved-roof monitors. The downhill side, facing a large valley and busy street, is a three-story "L" organized around a playground and community playing field.

The school and its site layout demonstrate a respect for the immediate neighborhood, for the natural topography, and for the larger community's needs for education and recreation facilities. P.S. 15 also exhibits a commitment to sustainable architecture and energy conservation by emphasizing natural lighting through large windows and skylight monitors, minimizing glare and heat load with perforated metal sun-shades, and using natural materials where possible. Community use of auditorium, gymnasium, and playing field help integrate school and neighborhood.

1

1 Three-story downhill side enclosing playground
  and playing field
2 Two-story uphill elevation respects adjoining
  homes
3 Floor plan of second floor

2

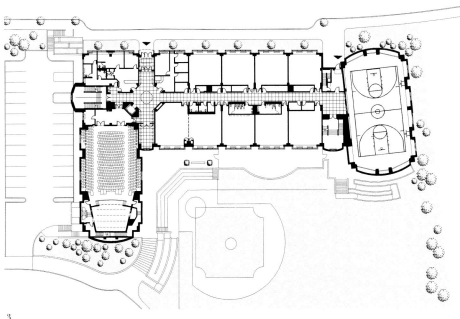

3

4 School and community auditorium
5 Gymnasium opens to playing field
6 "Commons" area for informal activities

4

5

6

Modular Schools/Mini-Schools

Design/Completion 1990/1999
Manhattan and Queens, New York
New York City Board of Education
New York City School Construction Authority
Steel structure, panelized construction, concrete slabs
Brick, metal roofing, metal windows

The urgent need for classrooms in New York and the difficulty in finding appropriate sites require alternate methods for siting and constructing schools. Two techniques have been successfully utilized to accelerate the delivery of school facilities:

Mini-Schools comprise small classroom buildings, usually linked to a larger "host" school which provides shared facilities—auditorium, gymnasium, and cafeteria. These mini-schools often serve early childhood requirements, while the host school cares for the upper grades. The small size of these structures is appropriate for the age group served, and allows them to be sited in school playgrounds, parking areas, or other sites adjoining existing schools.

Modular Schools are designed to be constructed either in the field, or pre-fabricated and delivered to the site in sections. The capability of construction either way increases competition among contractors, and often yields savings in cost and reductions in construction time. Construction techniques include metal-stud walls faced in masonry, concrete plank floors, pre-assembled plumbing, and other innovative procedures. Illustrated here is a Prototype Modular School and two Mini-Schools designed for New York City.

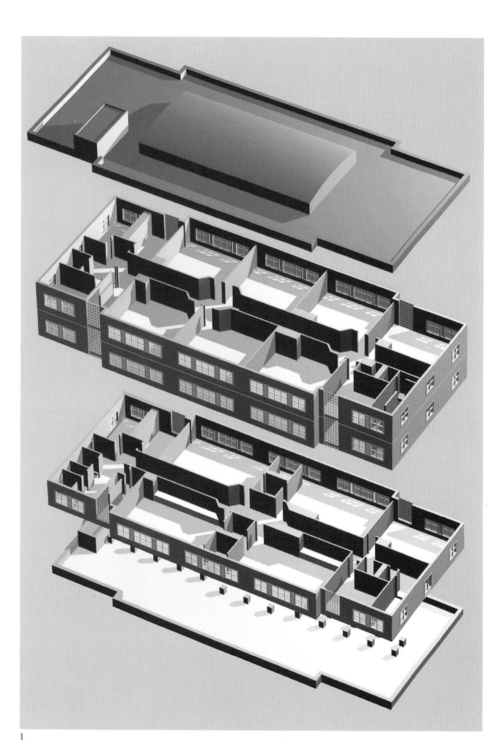

1

2

1 Prototype Modular School—exploded
 axonometric
2 P.S. 11 Mini-School adjoins host school
3 P.S. 11 street-level entrance
4 P.S. 128 corridor with skylight
5 P.S. 128 commons with administrative "house"

3

4

5

University/Library/Health Care

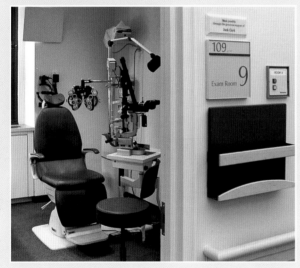

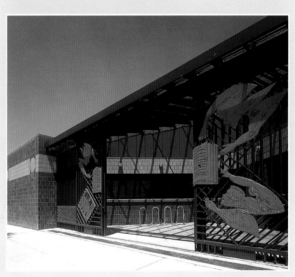

Richard Dattner & Partners Architects

Townsend Harris Hall, City College of New York

Design/Completion 1985/1990
New York, New York
City University of New York
7400 square meters
Steel frame, steel decks with concrete
Stone, terra-cotta trim, slate roof

This collegiate, gothic landmark, designed in 1905 by George W. Post, was reconfigured to house the School of Nursing, and learning centers for English and Mathematics. A new floor was inserted in an under-utilized auditorium, to create a realistic hospital training ward. Setting back the new intermediate floor from the landmarked exterior retained the high, gothic windows.

Nursing School offices occupy the new level over the teaching wards, with interior windows set back from the gothic fenestration. With new mechanical, life-safety, and electrical systems, the new construction encloses a modern, functional facility while respecting the fabric of the original building.

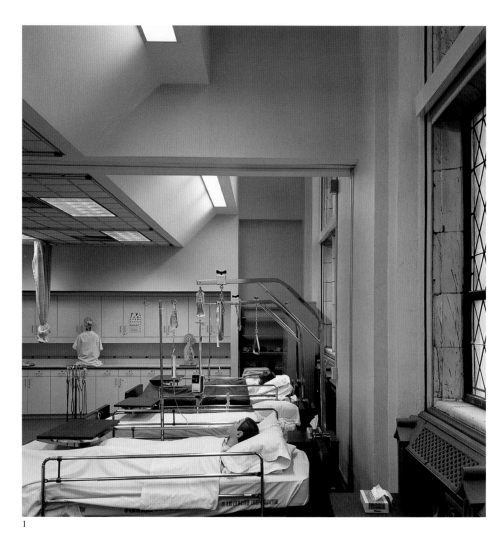

1

2

1   Hospital training ward, two-story gothic windows
2   Nursing School offices on inserted floor
3   Historic exterior was preserved
4   Historic interior features were restored

3

4

Boylan Hall Dining Facility, Brooklyn College

Design/Completion 1985/1988
Brooklyn, New York
City University of New York
Steel structure, concrete slabs

The flowering of public architecture during the Works Progress Administration gave Brooklyn, in 1937, a public college which expressed the duality of that time of contradictions. Dignified Georgian buildings define a landscaped quadrangle rivaling the Ivy League, while building interiors express a "Streamlined Modern" aesthetic of limited means and practical materials.

The renovation of the campus dining facility reflects this duality by establishing two design "voices"—a Streamlined Modern setting for students, and a Georgian Room for faculty dining and special events. The student dining hall, on the lower level of Boylan Hall, is organized around a central corridor renamed "Boylan Boulevard". Along this busy route are located the servery, dining areas, and an all-night diner. Since Brooklyn College is a commuter university, the student dining hall is also a meeting place, social hall, and study room. The Georgian Room reinforces the traditional, collegiate design of the campus, and is also a setting for meetings, conferences, and the display of art by students and faculty members.

1

1   Mural by Susan Davis brings the "quad" indoors
2   Boylan Boulevard organizes the student dining
     hall
3   The all-night diner and rotunda are a meeting
     place
4   The Georgian Room—under nine vaulted
     skylights

2

3

4

Columbia University School of Social Work

Design/Completion 1994/1996
New York, New York
Columbia University
1000 square meters
Steel structure, concrete slabs
Brick, tile, steel stair

The Columbia School of Social Work occupies McVickar Hall—a former apartment building near the main campus. The major shortcoming of this arrangement was the lack of a social gathering place for students and faculty. The solution was to enclose an unused rear yard to create a sky-lit, two-story atrium linking the first floor and basement levels. Opening the basement level to the atrium created a bright and spacious study area, lounge, and coffee bar on a formerly dark and under-utilized floor.

The first floor—the main entrance level to McVickar Hall—was renovated to provide seminar rooms, a student lounge/conference center, and a computer-learning center. A sculptural steel stair links the first and basement floors, with the original brick rear wall restored and left exposed. Two floors are now connected, and provide a social core for the entire facility.

1

1   Sky-lit atrium creates study area and lounge
2   Stair links first and basement levels

2

Parkchester Branch Library

Design/Completion 1982/1985
(Second Floor Addition 1999/2001)
Bronx, New York
The New York Public Library
New York City Department of Design and Construction
750 square meters (addition 500 square meters)
Steel structure, concrete slabs
Brick, steel columns, aluminum windows

Located on a busy commercial street with an elevated subway, this branch library provides books, computer access, and other learning materials to a community of elderly readers, newly arrived immigrants, and young children. The limited available resources are concentrated in one bold design gesture— a crescent-shaped entrance courtyard inhabited by artist Marcia Dalby's fiberglass kangaroo, dinosaur and frog. This form resolves several design goals: creating an appropriately important transition space between street and library; creating a safe reading and play space for children; allowing for a continuous, curved band of south-facing windows pulled back from the noisy street; and protecting the library precincts by a decorative fence. Library readers have daylight by which to read, and passersby can look into the library and be enticed, perhaps, to use it.

In the years since its completion, the library has experienced increasing use, and a second-floor addition is now planned in order to create a regional library. A slightly gentler curved façade will step back from the first floor— preserving the scale and openness of the entrance courtyard.

1

1   Under the elevated subway, a modestly
    monumental façade
2   Entrance gate to courtyard and library
3   Second-floor addition echoes curved façade
    of original building
4   Courtyard protects library and welcomes its users

2

3

4

Cypress Hills Branch Library

Design/Completion 1988/1992
Brooklyn, New York
Brooklyn Public Library
New York City Department of Design and Construction
750 square meters
Steel structure, concrete slabs
Brick, steel fence, aluminum windows

A beacon of civility and hope in one of New York's most troubled neighborhoods, this modest building turns inward to a central, two-story, sky-lit atrium. The organizing geometry of the interior is rotated 45 percent from the surrounding streets—adding to the contrast between the somewhat cloistered, peaceful interior and the protective masonry exterior of the library. Arrayed around the atrium are adult reading areas, a children's library, and computer stations with Internet access.

As in the Parkchester Branch Library (pp. 56-57), all windows face an enclosed entrance courtyard. Artist Rolando Briseño transformed the required entrance gates into highly visible public art that reflects the aspirations of community residents.

1

2

1 Entrance courtyard with gates by Rolando Briseño
2 Entrance façade both protects and welcomes users
3 Central atrium organizes the library

3

New York Presbyterian Eye Clinic

Design/Completion 1996/1999
New York, New York
New York Presbyterian Medical Center
600 square meters
Wood, plasterboard, composition tile

Replacing a venerable, but somewhat out-dated existing facility, the Flanzer Eye Clinic provides a state-of-the-art medical setting for diagnosis, treatment, and laser surgery. The clinic is organized with clear, unambiguous circulation, facilitating visually impaired people in finding their way. Soft, indirect lighting, muted colors, and control of daylight assist patients during the treatment and recovery process. Limited space for examining rooms required carefully coordinated, built-in cabinets to accommodate the required medical equipment.

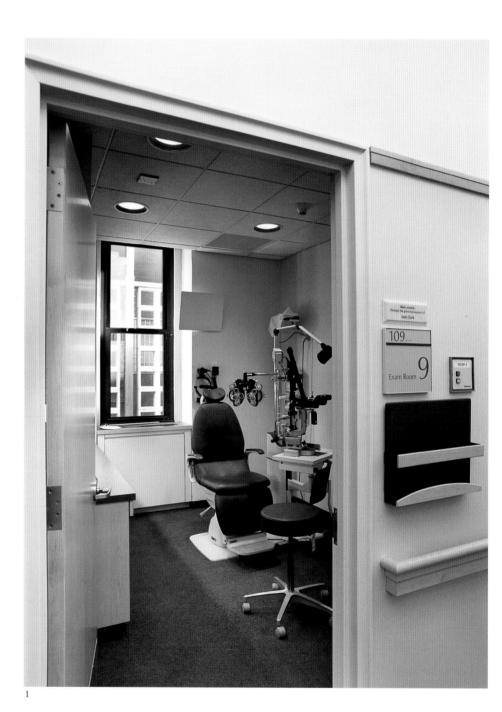

1

1   Examination/treatment rooms maximize available space
2   Corridors are visually emphasized to facilitate circulation
3   Lighting of waiting and recovery areas avoids glare and contrast

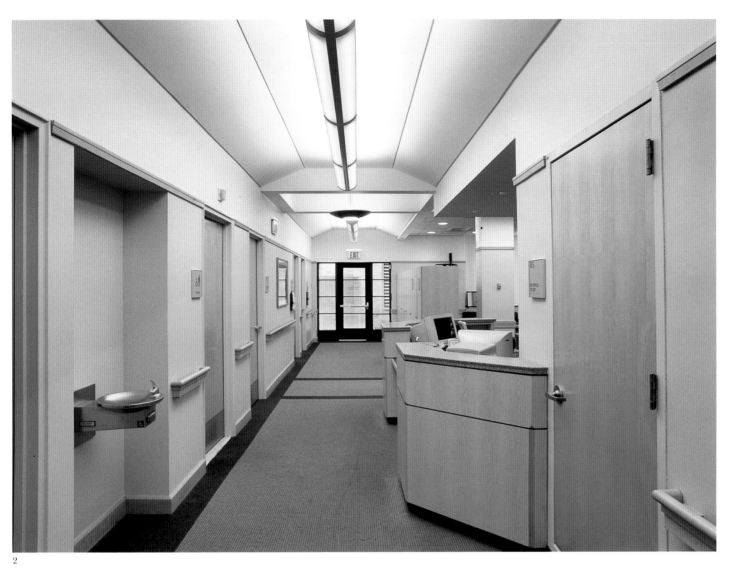

2

3

New York Presbyterian Pediatric Lung Center

Design/Completion 1996/1999
New York, New York
Children's and Babies' Hospital
New York Presbyterian Medical Center
1000 square meters
Wood, tile, plasterboard, porcelain tile, glass tile

Occupying the seventh floor of this existing hospital, the new Pediatric Lung Center creates a bright, cheerful, and inviting facility for the treatment of cystic fibrosis, asthma, and other childhood pulmonary conditions. Two main corridors—faced in porcelain tile panels—organize reception and playroom/waiting areas, evaluation laboratories, and individual physician office and examination rooms. The curved forms of the reception desk and wall linking the main corridors soften the rectilinear organization.

The waiting area adjoins a play area that has interactive toys, play surfaces, and computer/Internet stations. The major staff complaint refers (humorously) to the difficulty of luring children and parents away from this area.

1

1 Reception desk overlooks entrance and waiting area
2 Physician office and examination room
3 Waiting room and adjoining play room
4 Main corridor and curved reception desk and "umbrella"

2

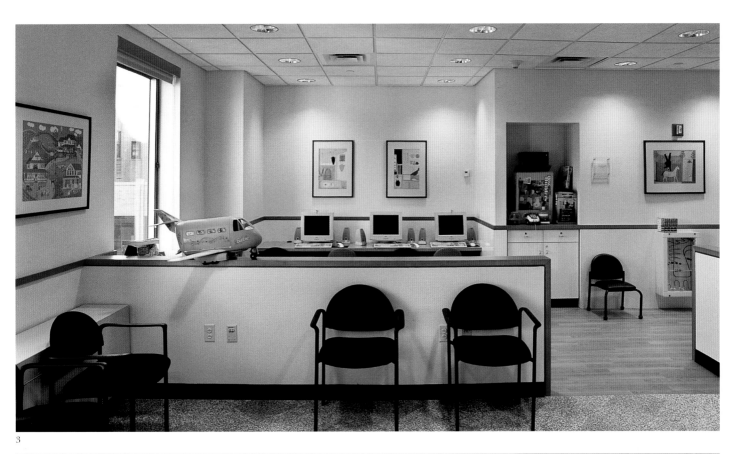

3

4

Sports/Fitness/Recreation

Richard Dattner & Partners Architects

Coney Island Lifeguard Stations

Design/Completion 1994/2002
Brooklyn, New York
US Army Corps of Engineers
New York City Parks and Recreation
14 Stations along 3 miles of beachfront
Concrete structure, pre-cast concrete roof
Concrete, masonry units, aluminum roofing

The Coney Island beaches annually host millions of New Yorkers who flock to the Atlantic Ocean. The historic boardwalk has been part of the New York City legend since the 19th century. As part of a Federal program of beach restoration, the existing, abandoned lifeguard stations and public rest rooms under the boardwalk will be replaced by 14 new structures.

These new pavilions—recalling the cabanas formerly populating the beaches—house lifeguard stations, first-aid facilities, and public rest rooms. Resembling inverted boats, these standardized structures also provide shelter from sun and rain, and a handicapped accessible entrance and transition from the boardwalk to the beach. Medallions with reliefs of marine animals enliven the buildings. At the primary public entrance to the beach at Stillwell Avenue, two pavilions are linked by an overhanging roof, to create an appropriately monumental entrance to the beach and ocean.

1

2

1   Stillwell Avenue pavilions create the main beach entrance
2   Typical pavilions provide shade and beach accessibility
3   New pavilions adjoining the historic Parachute Jump

3

Louis Armstrong Cultural Center

Design/Completion 1987/1993
Queens, New York
ELMCOR Community Organization
New York City Department of Design and Construction
3000 square meters
Steel frame, steel decks with concrete
Brick, steel pipe canopy, aluminum windows

Adjoining the historic Louis Armstrong home, the Elmhurst/Corona community organization operates this multi-purpose neighborhood center. The Louis Armstrong Cultural Center hosts local and national basketball tournaments in a two-story court accommodating 750 spectators. This large gymnasium—partially below grade to preserve the community scale—is also used for volleyball, gymnastics, martial arts, dance, and theatrical productions. A translucent canopy shelters spectators awaiting entry.

Other floors house classrooms, senior citizens' activities, and arts and crafts shops. An early-childhood center opens onto a rooftop recreation terrace over the main gymnasium. Two indoor handball/racquetball courts are located on the top floor.

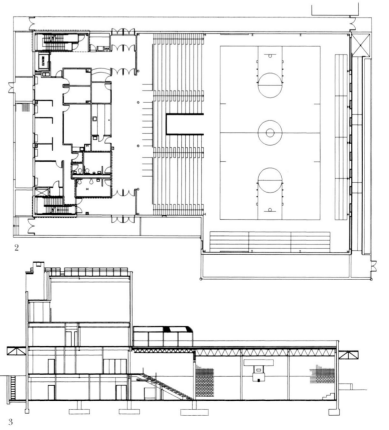

1

2

3

1 Façade is enlivened by "jazzy" diagonal stripes
2 Plan of entrance level
3 Section through major spaces
4 Gymnasium is a flexible, multi-purpose space
5 Spectators enter at top, participants on the lower level

4

5

Asphalt Green AquaCenter

Design/Completion 1989/1994
New York, New York
Asphalt Green Incorporated
New York City Parks and Recreation
7500 square meters
Steel frame, concrete pool and canopies
Brick, concrete, window walls

A unique partnership between a group of dedicated philanthropists and New York City resulted in the development of the city's leading aquatic facility—on a difficult triangular site wedged between a city playground, sanitation ramp, and the F.D.R. Drive. Asphalt Green (named for the parabolic, former asphalt plant) operates the facility at no cost to the city— by charging 70 percent of its users and providing free public access to 30 percent of its programs.

The core of the AquaCenter is a 50-meter, 8-lane, Olympic-standard pool with state-of-the-art competition gutters and re-circulation systems. The pool can be divided into three zones by floating movable bulkheads—creating a 50-meter-long-course venue or two 25-yard pools. An hydraulic, movable floor can vary the depth of one end of the pool from 2 meters to floor-deck level for handicapped access and swimming instruction, and a large underwater window is available for observation and instruction. Seven hundred spectators can be accommodated at swimming meets and diving competitions at one and 3-meter levels. Upper levels of the AquaCenter house fitness floors and administrative offices for the five-acre Asphalt Green campus.

1

Asphalt Green

1 Concrete waves greet swimmers and visitors
2 Asphalt Green logo, designed by Donovan & Green
3 Waving façade softens the building's impact on the adjoining park
4 AquaCenter wedged between highway, ramp, and playground

2

3

4

5   South wall, facing playing field
6   Section through pool and activity floors
Opposite:
    Curved steel trusses enclose pool
Following pages:
    Asphalt Plant and AquaCenter along F.D.R. Drive

5

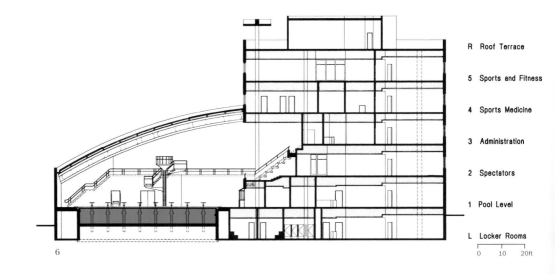

R Roof Terrace

5 Sports and Fitness

4 Sports Medicine

3 Administration

2 Spectators

1 Pool Level

L Locker Rooms

6

0   10   20ft

Riverbank State Park

Design/Completion 1978/1993
New York, New York
New York State Office of Parks, Recreation and Historic Preservation
New York City Department of Environmental Protection
Site: 28.5 acres. Buildings: 19,690 square meters
Steel frame, tile and metal wall panels
Steel, tile, metal cladding, aluminum windows

Riverbank State Park represents the successful transformation of an unwanted but necessary public facility (the North River Pollution Treatment Plant) into an intensively used community resource—Riverbank is the second-busiest state park in New York—visited by almost 4 million persons annually. Occupying the 28.5-acre roof of the sewage plant, the park provides recreation resources for the Manhattan community: a 50-meter indoor swimming pool; a covered skating rink (ice skating in winter, roller-blading in warm weather); a multi-purpose cultural center; a multi-use athletics building for basketball, volleyball, and gymnastics; and a restaurant and carousel.

Two bridges provide pedestrian, bus, and emergency vehicle access to Riverbank—there is no automobile access except for taxis and the disabled. Outdoor facilities include a 25-yard swimming pool, riverfront amphitheater, boat landing, and 23 acres of playing fields, picnic areas, riverfront promenades, and children's playgrounds.

Superimposing five structures, two bridges, and playing fields over the 14-section roof of an operating sewage plant required coordination of every design and construction operation with the supporting plant. The weight of the park buildings, roadways, and landscaping was calculated to comply with loading limits for each roof section, and the required expansion joints were major design determinants.

1

1   Stair/elevator access to riverfront amphitheater
    and boat landing
2   Riverbank resembles an aircraft carrier in the
    Hudson River
Opposite:
    Park entrance, skating rink, and cultural center

2

4   Entrance lobby to interior recreation facilities
5   Gymnasium accommodates a variety of activities
6   50-meter pool, divisible into three zones
7   Water play area and amphitheater
Following pages:
   Illuminated skylights invite night-time visitors

4

5

6

7

Pottruck Health and Fitness Center, University of Pennsylvania

Design/Completion 1999/2001
Philadelphia, Pennsylvania
The University of Pennsylvania
6500 square meters
Steel frame, steel decks with concrete
Steel, metal panels, aluminum window walls

The David S. Pottruck Health and Fitness Center joins the existing Gimbel Gym and Sheerr Pool to complete a comprehensive recreation and wellness complex for the entire university community. The new building is a series of largely open "trays", supporting areas for weight training, exercise, yoga, dance, aerobics, and other fitness activities. The existing pool and gymnasium are being rehabilitated, with new locker rooms on the basement level supporting both new and existing buildings.

Rather than attaching to the existing structure, the new fitness center sets back to enclose an interior "street"—a campus walk within a sky-lit atrium—linking both buildings. All the activities are visible from this atrium, with a cascading stair providing access to the fitness floors and the bridge to the upper-level gymnasium. The fitness levels step back on each floor—and cantilever over the exterior campus walk—in order to allow the maximum daylight to reach both interior and exterior streets. Open balconies at the upper levels overlook a climbing wall suspended from the former exterior wall of Gimbel Gym.

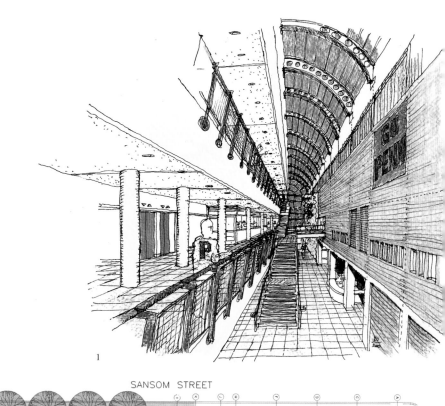

1

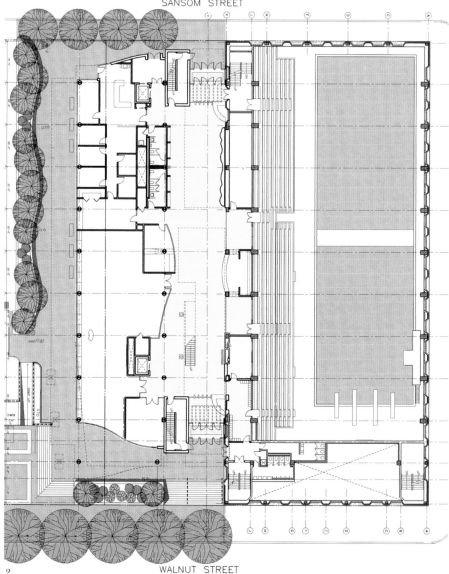

2

1   Atrium creates an interior campus walk
2   Entrance level links new and existing buildings
3   Atrium section showing cascading stair and open
    balconies
4   Section through Fitness Center (left) and existing
    gym (right)

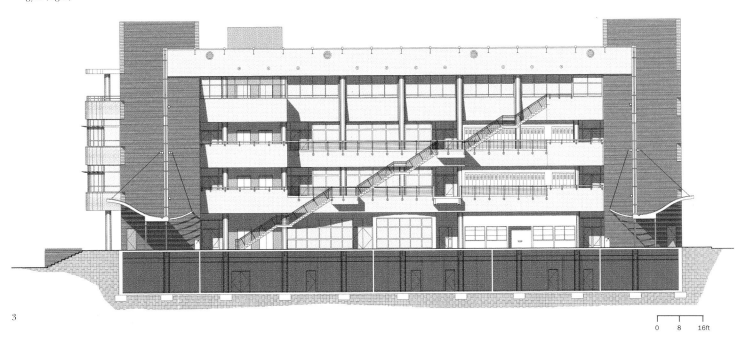

3

0   8   16ft

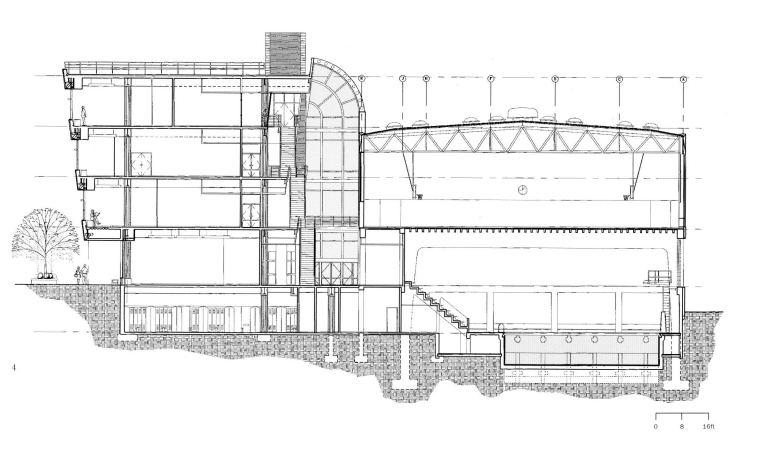

4

0   8   16ft

Goodwill Games Swimming and Diving Complex

Design/Completion 1994/1998
East Meadow, New York
New York State Dormitory Authority
Nassau County Parks and Recreation
7600 square meters
Concrete buttresses and pool, steel arch trusses, tensile fabric
Steel, metal panels, masonry, aluminum windows

The aquatic center built to host the 1998 Goodwill Games addresses two major design goals—to insert a large structure sensitively into a natural park, and to design a sports facility that can host a world-class event and then revert to a year-round community recreation facility. The first goal is met by partially earth-sheltering the pool level, and enclosing the facility under a curved roof. The second goal is accomplished by providing a south façade which can be raised to provide 1600 temporary seats to supplement the 2000 permanent seats during major events. The site is shaped to allow at-grade access to both the lower pool and locker level, and the upper spectator/lounge level.

Continued

1

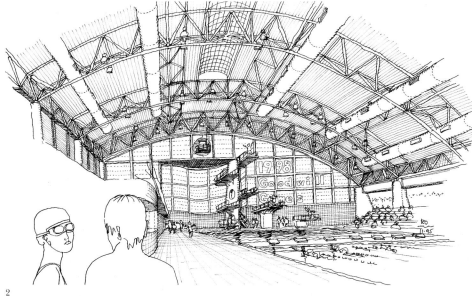

2

84

1 Landscaped berm leads to spectator entrance
2 Architect's original sketch of pool interior
3 Masonry base with pool-level entrance

3

Concrete buttresses support eight curved steel trusses which span 46 meters (150 ft.) over the pool and indoor seating. The competition pool is one of the largest in the world, measuring 71 meters (233 ft.) by 25 meters (82 ft.), in order to accommodate simultaneous 50-meter swimming, and diving at one 3, 5, 7.5, and 10-meter levels. Special pool features include a movable floor, two movable bulkheads, and state-of-the-art gutter and surge tank systems. The diving well includes water bubblers, sparger system, and a spa pool for the divers.

Opposite:
View of pool, diving platforms, central skylight

5 Tensile fabric overhang controls sunlight
6 Concrete diving platform support echoes buttresses
7 Building volume is minimized to respect natural setting

5

6

7

Berkeley Carroll School Athletic Center

Design/Completion 1995/2000
Brooklyn, New York
The Berkeley Carroll School
1860 square meters
Steel frame, concrete slabs and pool
Brick, aluminum windows

The Berkeley Carroll School—presently occupying three sites in Park Slope—required additional facilities for recreation and athletics. A large, independent school gymnasium and pool center was gracefully inserted into the historic Park Slope streetscape by enclosing it within a three-part façade resembling the scale of adjacent townhouses. The gymnasium and bleachers occupy the street and mezzanine levels, the pool and lockers are below grade, and the top floor windows shield a roof playground. The new building is linked internally to the adjoining lower school.

1

2

1   Tripartite façade encloses pool, gym, and roof playground
2   Roof playground for young children
3   School gymnasium is also an assembly space
4   25-yard swimming pool under gymnasium

3

4

Jewish Community Center of Staten Island

Design/Completion 1998/2001
Staten Island, New York
The Jewish Community Center of Staten Island
9800 square meters
Steel frame, steel decks with concrete, masonry and stone walls
Stone, masonry, metal panels, aluminum windows

The Jewish Community Center of Staten Island is a community provider of social and recreational services for all age groups. On a site adjoining a protected greenbelt, the new facility is a "village" of four structures, arranged in a pinwheel around a central atrium. Four organizing walls—of Learning, Life, Community, and Remembrance—define the four major functions: early childhood school, gymnasium and fitness center, swimming pool, and social hall. The center also houses a library, crafts shops, a café, and administrative offices.

A "Tree of Life" canopy set into the curved Wall of Welcome leads visitors into the central hall and atrium forming the social heart of the center—a place from which the activities of all the quadrants can be experienced.

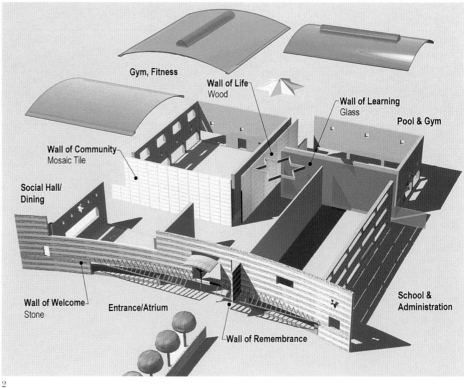

1

2

1 The Jewish Community Center, seen from Manor Road
2 Five walls organize the major activity areas
3 Curved Wall of Welcome with overhanging social hall roof

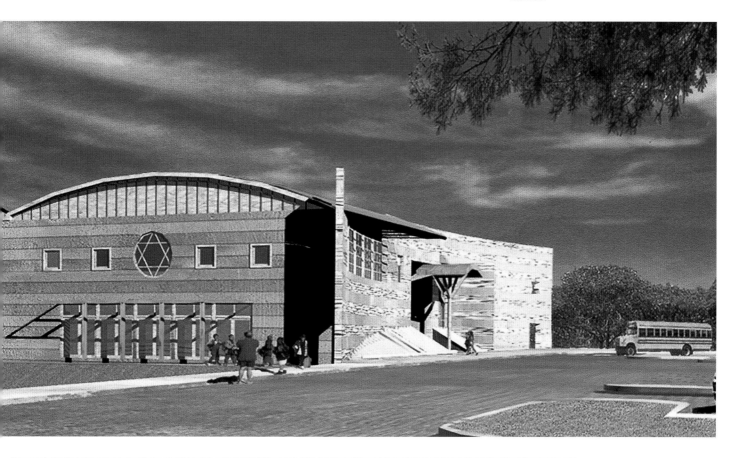

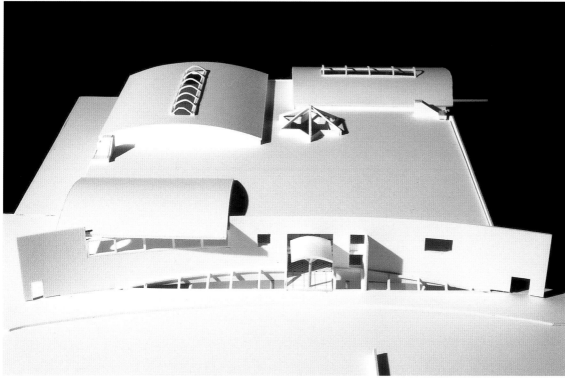

3

New York Athletic Club Pool

Design/Completion 1995/1998
The New York Athletic Club
3500 square meters
Steel frame, steel pool, concrete slabs
Tile, plaster, stainless steel, aluminum windows

Three floors of the historic, 1927 New York Athletic Club building on Central Park South were completely rehabilitated to create a modern aquatic facility and central locker rooms serving the athletic spaces throughout the building. The pool deck was extended to provide views of Central Park, by relocating the sauna and steam rooms, and building two new spa pools within a raised platform. The former spectator balcony was transformed into a glass-enclosed, air-conditioned lounge overlooking the pool.

New windows, lighting, ceramic tiles, and climate control have turned this facility into one of the premier swimming pools in New York.

1

2

1 Enclosed balcony overlooks swimming pool
2 New lounge area with Central Park views
3 The transformed pool under a vaulted ceiling
4 Wall tile "pixels" enliven the walls of pool area

3

4

Gathering/Celebration

Richard Dattner & Partners Architects

Lawrence A. Wien Stadium, Columbia University

Design/Completion 1979/1984
New York, New York
Columbia University
15,000 spectators
Cast and precast concrete structure

The Lawrence A. Wien Stadium replaces
the legendary 50,000-seat wooden stadium
which served Columbia University since
1927. Built on Columbia's 27-acre
Baker Field in upper Manhattan, and
overlooking the Harlem River and
New Jersey Palisades, the new facility
is responsive to community concerns.
It allows off-hour community use of the
running track. In order to minimize
the stadium's visual impact on the
surrounding residential community,
the home stand structure is partially on-
grade—taking advantage of a natural
slope and lowering the profile of the
stadium complex.

The on-grade seats are cast in place, with
upper sections of the stadium built of pre-
cast concrete. A three-level press box, VIP
lounge, and observation roof, reached
by elevator and stairs, also hosts campus
events in a setting with spectacular views.
In addition to inter-collegiate football,
the Wien Stadium is the setting for major
track and field competitions, and has been
designated as the Field Hockey venue
in New York City's bid for the 2012
Olympic Games.

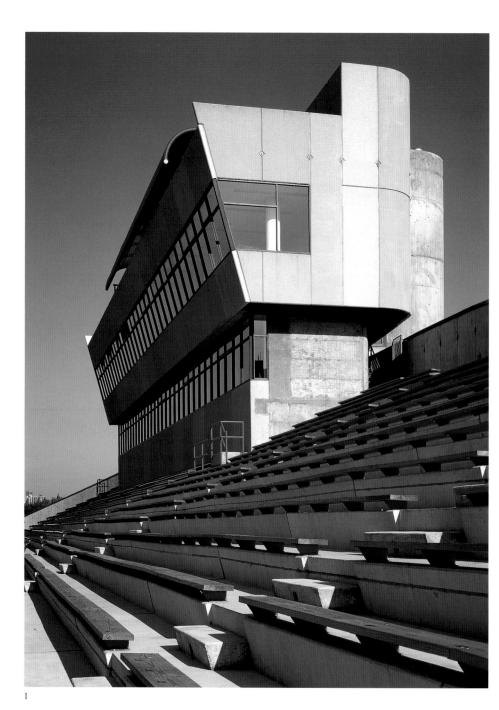

1

1   Press box on upper level, VIP lounge on lower
2   Home stands seat 10,000 spectators
3   Section through home stands
Following pages:
    Concourse with elevator and stairs to press box

2

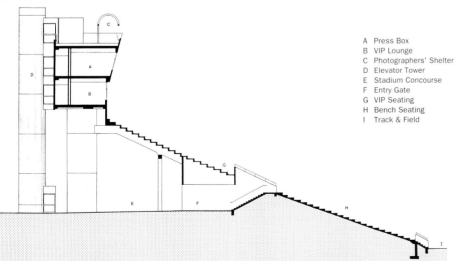

A   Press Box
B   VIP Lounge
C   Photographers' Shelter
D   Elevator Tower
E   Stadium Concourse
F   Entry Gate
G   VIP Seating
H   Bench Seating
I   Track & Field

3

Stony Brook Stadium
State University of New York at Stony Brook

Design/Completion 1997/2001
Stony Brook, New York
State University of New York at Stony Brook
State University Construction Fund
7500 Spectators
Cast in place and pre-cast concrete structure

This multi-use stadium will accommodate an initial 7500 spectators, with provision for expansion to 15,000. In order to minimize visual impact to the park-like campus, two-thirds of the seats will be on-grade around an excavated "bowl". Planted earth berms surrounding the playing field reinforce the relationship between building and landscape. The upper levels of the home stands connect with an elevated press box, VIP level, and observation roof—sheltering a primary campus walk below. The stadium grounds will remain open to campus circulation when events are not being held.

A field house is built under the south spectator stands, containing team lockers, weight and training rooms, and related sports facilities. Stony Brook selected a synthetic playing surface to allow inter-collegiate and intra-mural football, lacrosse, and soccer events to be held in any weather.

1

1   Main stands with press box, VIP level, observation roof
2   Cross section through main stands and "bowl"
3   Playing field, looking toward campus center
4   Campus walk under main stands

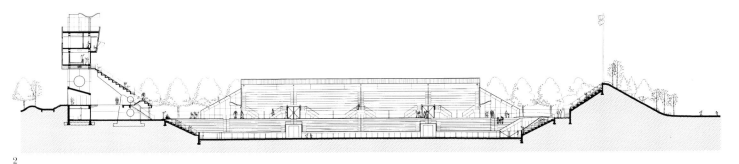

2

3

4

Whitney Museum of American Art Exhibition

Design/Completion 1994
New York, New York
Whitney Museum of American Art
800 square meters
Stone floors, plasterboard partitions

The Whitney Museum's annual exhibition of painting, sculpture, and photography from their permanent collection was installed on the fourth floor of their Marcel Breuer-designed building. The trapezoidal Breuer windows were restored to view and were visually integrated to complement the exhibition. A new grid—shifted slightly from the existing geometry—organizes the exhibition in a "pinwheel" around a serene center gallery exhibiting "The Islands" paintings of Agnes Martin. Art works installed in the areas around this central space display the variety and depth of the Whitney Museum's permanent collection.

1

2

1   An exterior window is glimpsed from each gallery
2   Work by Sarah Charlesworth, Ad Reinhardt, Tony
    Smith
3   Work by Nan Goldin, Charles Ray
4   Work by Philip Taaffe, Ellsworth Kelly, Barnet
    Newman, Frank Stella

3

4

Intrepid Park and Museum

Design 1985
New York, New York
Intrepid Museum Foundation
33,500 square meters
Concrete pier structures, floating barges

The historic World War II aircraft carrier *USS Intrepid,* moored at Pier 86 on the Hudson River, is a museum complex exhibiting warships, aircraft, and related equipment, and is a memorial to the men and women who fought at sea. In order to expand the focus of this waterfront complex, a design was commissioned to develop the adjacent pier as an educational, science-based theme park and museum.

Pier 85 would contain restaurants, public boardwalks, and commercial space—similar to South Street Seaport. Four exhibit barges—organized around the themes of Water, Earth, Air, and Space—would be fabricated off-site and towed to a permanent berth at this pier. The exhibits would stress environmental themes, to balance the existing military display, suggesting that the next struggle might be to preserve our natural world.

1

1   Exhibition barges cluster around recreation/
    restaurant pier
2   Retractable bridge links Piers 85 and 86
Opposite:
    Intrepid complex anchors new midtown
    development

2

© 1988 RICHARD DATTNER

Democratic National Convention

Design/Completion 1991/1992
Madison Square Garden, New York, New York
Democratic National Convention Committee
New York City Economic Development Corporation
36,000 square meters
Steel structure, plywood platforms
Plasterboard, carpet, video wall

As part of New York City's hosting of the 1992 Democratic National Convention, the interior of Madison Square Garden was extensively (and temporarily) renovated to house the 25,000 delegates, commentators, reporters, and camera operators who attended the four-day event. Architectural services included design of the podium structure, press, and camera platforms, and the coordination of power, lighting, communications, and security systems. Heading a team of architects, stage designers, lighting, graphics, and electrical consultants, our firm coordinated the timely design and delivery of this complex project.

The podium was designed as a public plaza linked to the Convention floor by a series of accessible, curved steps. Patterned after Rome's Porta Di Ripetta (designed in 1703 by Alessandro Specchi, the designer of the Spanish Steps), the Democratic podium was a democratic place of arrival, public gathering, and spectacle. At selected moments, the rostrum was lowered to the level of the podium floor—eliminating any physical barrier between candidate and delegate.

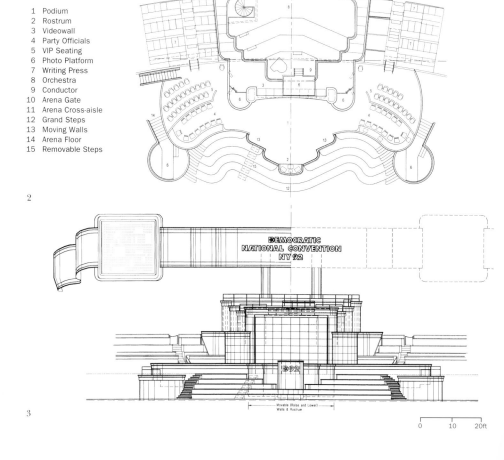

1

1   Podium
2   Rostrum
3   Videowall
4   Party Officials
5   VIP Seating
6   Photo Platform
7   Writing Press
8   Orchestra
9   Conductor
10 Arena Gate
11 Arena Cross-aisle
12 Grand Steps
13 Moving Walls
14 Arena Floor
15 Removable Steps

2

3

1 Delegates' view of podium
2 Plan of podium, steps, and camera platforms
3 Elevation showing video wall, overhead banner,
   and screens
4 Convention graphics by Service Station
5 The Clinton/Gore slate is elected

Rainbow Bridge U.S. Plaza

Design 1990
Niagara Falls, New York
U.S. Customs/Hardesty & Hanover Engineers
4200 square meters
Steel structure, concrete slabs, GFRC wall panels
Steel, concrete, window walls

The Rainbow Bridge at Niagara Falls is one of the busiest border crossings into the United States; massive traffic tie-ups are experienced each summer. This competition entry demonstrated that a federal building could be dignified, festive, and welcoming, without resorting to the formal monumentality characterizing many "official" structures.

Canadian guests are greeted with a friendly wave from a gently undulating building faced in glass-reinforced concrete panels and supported entirely by a double row of structural flagpoles.

Flags waving in the border breezes and gently waving walls establish a festive note, while the electronic billboard imparts information and fragments of our written heritage to entering and departing visitors.

1

1 Gently undulating façade suspended from
   structural flagpoles
2 Original concept sketch

Living/Shelter

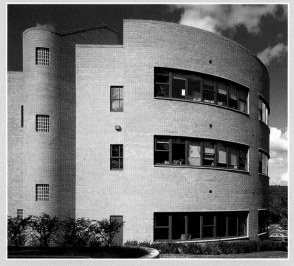

Richard Dattner & Partners Architects

Administration for Children's Services, Children's Center

Design/Completion 1997/2000
New York, New York
New York City Administration for Children's Services
New York City Department of Design & Construction
12,600 square meters
Steel frame, concrete and terra cotta slabs
Brick, terra cotta, aluminum windows

Bellevue Hospital's historic R & S building, designed by McKim, Mead & White in 1903, is being transformed into the flagship facility of the Administration for Children's Services (ACS). The restoration of the brick and terra cotta exterior, and the Guastavino vaulted ceilings, will bring this important landmark to its former prominence, while a total reconstruction of the interior will create a comprehensive facility for the troubled children under the care of ACS.

Children are brought into the center through a protected entrance off a private drive, to a reception and screening area. The children's entrance level also houses specialists in finding placements for these children in foster homes or institutional settings. Dedicated elevators take those children requiring temporary accommodation to the 2nd floor (young children) and 3rd floor (teenagers). A new public entrance on First Avenue serves the conference center and auditorium on the main floor. The 4th, 5th, and 6th floors house the Satterwhite Training Academy—where ACS staff receive special training in working with children and their families.

1

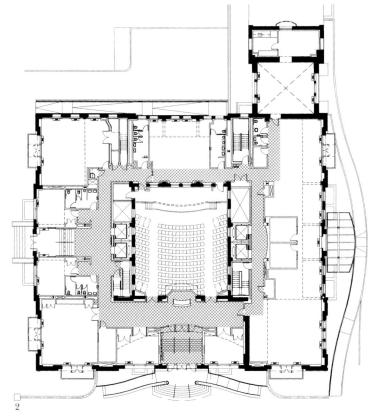

2

1   First Avenue elevation of Children's Center
2   Plan of conference-center level
3   Children's entrance (right) and public
    entrance (left)
4   New entrance canopy respects original
    architecture

3

4

Leake & Watts School and Residences

Design/Completion 1993/1998
Yonkers, New York
Leake & Watts Family Services, Inc.
(Carlo Zaskorski, Associated Architect)
School: 7000 square meters
Steel frame, concrete slabs
Brick, metal roofing, window walls

Leake & Watts, established as an orphanage in 1831, has raised thousands of children to responsible adulthood, and continues its work with troubled teenagers orphaned by drug-addicted or otherwise absent parents. The core of the Leake & Watts community is a new school tucked into a hillside. It serves both residents and additional pupils from the surrounding community. The curved school façade allows most classrooms to face the river. The north wing contains classrooms, laboratories, shops, a library, and dining facility, while the south wing contains the social and sporting activity spaces, which can serve the community after school hours.

The three new "villages", each comprising three cottages clustered around a village green, and two restored cottages, house 154 residents on the Olmsted-designed grounds. Residents live in a cottage for 14 children (ages 12–19) and two resident counselors, with front porch "stoops" forming a transition between cottage and village. Mature trees, stone walls, and other site features are carefully preserved. The orderly layout, serene landscape, and views of the Hudson River create a refuge from urban chaos for the average 18-month tenure of a resident.

1

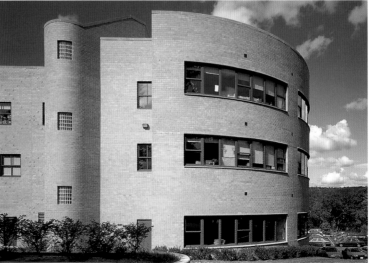

1   Three-story façade of school faces Hudson River
2   Curved end of classroom wing
3   Floor plan of entrance (middle) level
4   Uphill, two-story façade with school entrance

2

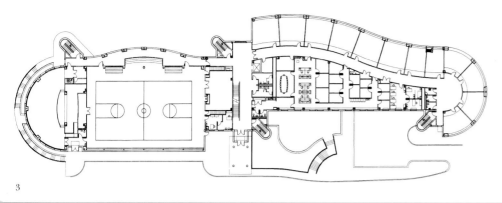

3

4

5

6

5 Residential villages are clustered around existing trees
6 Residential village, administration building in background
7 First-floor plan of residential cottage
8 Second-floor plan showing single and double rooms

118

7

8

Roundtop at Montrose

Design/Completion 1992/2001
Montrose, New York
Triglia Development
92 residential units, 18 acres
Metal stud construction, wood cladding

Located on a sloping, densely wooded site about one hour from New York City, this low-rise apartment development is patterned after the 18th-century Royal Crescent in Bath, England. The 92 residential units are linked in a serpentine curve winding through the site, respecting the topography and retaining a spectacular stand of Norway Spruce trees. By clustering the residences and related parking on 2.5 acres, 86 percent of this unique site is preserved as a natural area. The Roundtop complex adjoins a commuter rail station. It demonstrates a strategy for sustainable development— conserving resources while providing needed housing for young families and retired couples.

The existing slope is utilized to provide convenient access and spectacular views for the stacked duplex units—the upper duplex also contains a sleeping loft. All units share a central clubhouse, swimming pool, and children's playground. Nature trails and a sewage treatment facility are located elsewhere on the site.

1

Rear Elevation

0 2 4ft

2

3

1　　Residential crescent winds through the woods
2　　Elevation of four-apartment segment
3　　Section through stacked duplex apartments
4　　Site plan

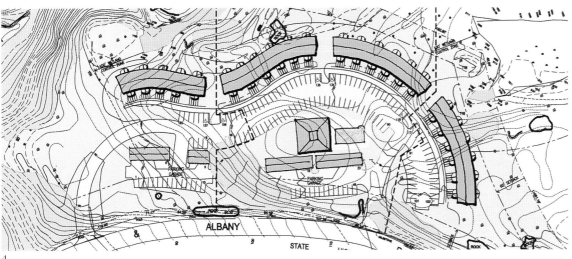

4

River View Gardens

Design/Completion 1996/2001
Queens, New York
New York Foundation for Senior Citizens
U.S. Dept. of Housing and Urban Development
Queens West Development Corporation
7400 square meters
Masonry-bearing walls, pre-cast concrete floors
Brick, cast-stone base and trim, aluminum windows

River View Gardens is the latest in a series of Federally funded, affordable senior residences designed for the New York Foundation for Senior Citizens. To be built as part of the new Queens West neighborhood being developed along the East River, River View's residents will have spectacular views of Manhattan. A terrace on the roof of the adjoining residential and parking structure will provide a landscaped open space.

The new, eight-story building contains 79 one-bedroom apartments, lobby, lounge, community room and kitchen, activity and work rooms, an apartment for the resident superintendent, and other resident facilities. The handsomely furnished public spaces and carpeted hallways create a dignified and inviting residential setting for both residents and staff.

1

1   River View Gardens faces a public plaza and riverfront park
2   Plan of typical residential floor
3   River View and adjoining Avalon Development (Perkins, Eastman Architects)
4   Conceptual sketch

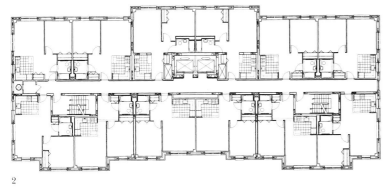

2

3

4

Clinton Gardens

Design/Completion 1990/1993
New York, New York
New York Foundation for Senior Citizens
U.S. Dept. of Housing and Urban Development
8400 square meters
Masonry-bearing walls, pre-cast concrete floors
Brick, cast-stone base and trim, aluminum windows

This apartment building, for low-income elderly residents, responds to the special zoning of the Clinton neighborhood, which mandated a 10-story building with a setback at the seventh floor to match the scale of West 54th Street. In order to accommodate 100 residential units on a limited site, the community room, kitchen, arts and crafts spaces, and laundry are located in the basement. By excavating the garden level one floor below grade, the basement became a second ground floor, providing sunlight into the communal spaces on that level, as well as direct access from these spaces to the south-facing garden.

A small beauty parlor is a popular amenity, as are a variety of classes and social activities which help residents organize their days and remain active. Communal meals are served daily to residents unable to prepare their own. Residents who are frail receive assistance with shopping, cooking, and other household tasks.

1

1   Sunken garden level brings daylight into basement
2   West 54th Street elevation steps back at 7th floor
3   Entrance-level floor plan

2

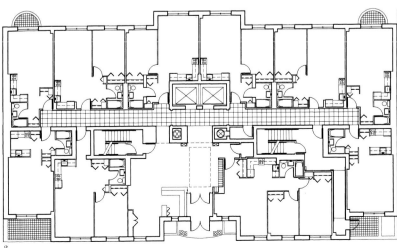

3

Ridge Street Gardens

Design/Completion 1990/1992
New York, New York
New York Foundation for Senior Citizens
U.S. Dept. of Housing and Urban Development
8600 square meters
Masonry-bearing walls, pre-cast concrete floors
Brick, cast-stone base and trim, aluminum windows

The seven-story building houses 100 apartments for older people, in the historic Lower East Side of Manhattan. A columned entrance canopy dignifies the simple and efficient linear structure. The social center of the building—entrance lobby, lounge, community room, and kitchen—is clustered around the intersection of the entrance and the elevators, the busy focus for daily activities. An attendant at the lobby security desk monitors the entrance, assists residents, and is electronically linked to each apartment.

The high level of interior design at the public spaces is a hallmark of the sponsor, providing residents with a much-appreciated, home-like setting. The enclosed garden is designed with comparable attention to detail, including game tables, seating, and a variety of trees and flowers cared for by residents.

1   Columned portico announces the main entrance
2   Entrance and garden-level floor plan
3   Lobby desk is a focus for social activity
4   Lounge interior is typical of communal spaces

1

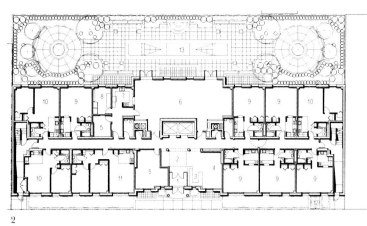

Ground Floor
1　Vestibule
2　Lobby
3　Security
4　Lounge
5　Office
6　Community Room
7　Kitchen
8　Storage
9　0-Bedroom Unit
10　1-Bedroom Unit
11　2-Bedroom Unit
12　Sidewalk Lift
13　Garden

0　10　20ft　N

2

3

4

Commerce/Research/Distribution

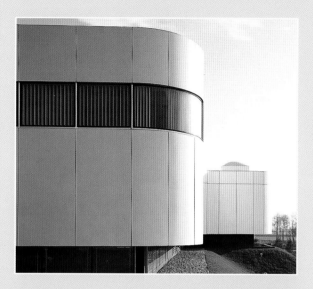

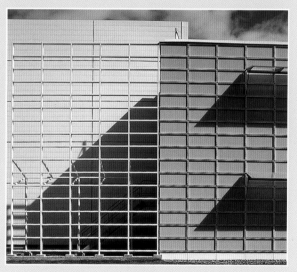

Richard Dattner & Partners Architects

Estée Lauder Corporate Headquarters

Design/Completion 1989/1995
New York, New York
Estée Lauder Companies
(Joint Venture with Davis, Brody & Associates)
15,600 square meters
Metal, glass, wood, carpet

Planning for this corporate headquarters was approached as a city-planning exercise, with interior streets, plazas, traffic nodes, and commons organizing a work environment for 1000 executives and creative staff. Within the building's long, narrow floor plate, the design balances corporate consistency with the individuality of the subsidiary companies— *Clinique* is white and clinical, *Prescriptives* is hip and urbane, *Origins* is woodsy and natural, *Aramis* is masculine, and *Estée Lauder* blends tradition and modernity.

For each of the six floors, a circulation spine rings the floor, and functions as a gallery for the display of a significant art collection. Natural light is maximized for the entire staff by using glass partitions and reserving corner spaces for shared "commons" conference rooms. Specialized departments include creative studios, videoconferencing facilities, display and presentation rooms, legal, office services, and other support departments. The project spanned a five-year period, to allow for construction with the minimum disruption of existing offices.

1

2

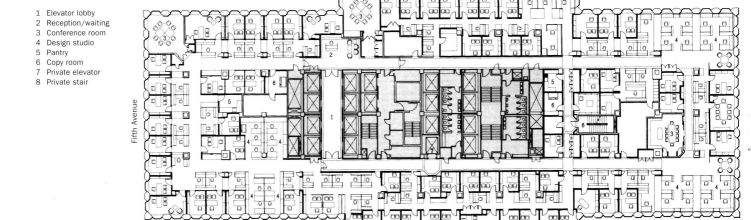

1   Elevator lobby
2   Reception/waiting
3   Conference room
4   Design studio
5   Pantry
6   Copy room
7   Private elevator
8   Private stair

59th Street

Fifth Avenue

58th Street

0   10   25ft

3

4

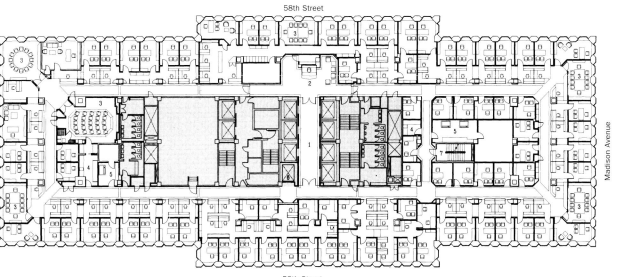

58th Street

Madison Avenue

58th Street

6 Office of Chief Executive Officer
7 Corner "commons" conference area
8 Office of Chief Executive Officer
9 Estée Lauder reception salon at executive floor

6

7

8

9

Estée Lauder Laboratories

Design/Completion 1964/1972
Melville, New York
Estée Lauder Companies
(Joint Venture with Davis, Brody & Associates)
30,000 square meters
Steel structure, concrete slabs
Steel porcelain panels, glass, concrete

One of the first large buildings to use porcelain-coated steel panels, this office, laboratory, manufacturing, and storage building also pioneered curved panels and glass set into neoprene gaskets. The wall-panel system was designed to be demountable, in order to accommodate future expansion for this rapidly growing company—within four years the building doubled in size.

Designed to be legible at high speed from an adjoining expressway, the building is partially earth-sheltered behind grass berms, to minimize its bulk and integrate building and landscape on this former sod farm. This strategy also minimized energy use, allowing a subsequent adjacent building to be heated by the original heating plant.

1

1   Curved metal panels and glazing at corners
2   Earth berms screen lower levels from adjoining
    expressway
3   Enclosed courtyard adjoining cafeteria
Following pages:
    View from the expressway

2

3

Estée Lauder Automated Storage Retrieval Facility

Design/Completion 1976/1980
Melville, New York
Estée Lauder Companies
(Joint Venture with Davis, Brody & Associates)
16,000 square meters
Steel structure, concrete slabs and retaining walls
Steel and fiberglass panels

An early example of a computer-controlled warehouse and distribution center, this facility is linked by an enclosed conveyor and personnel bridge to an adjoining manufacturing facility (see pp. 136–139). In order to respect the semi-rural nature of the site, conserve energy, and comply with town height limits, the 21-meter-high building is one-third below grade. Pallets of raw materials are received at protected truck bays, and are carried by conveyor belts to the manufacturing facility for processing and assembly. Finished goods are returned to the Automated Storage Retrieval Facility for storage in the high-bay automated warehouse—from where they are retrieved, picked, packed, and shipped.

Above-grade walls are clad in horizontal, deep-rib steel panels, and earth berms cover the 7-meter-high concrete retaining walls. Curved panels fabricated in fiberglass carry the ribs around corners, define the main entrance, enclose stairs, and cover emergency air intakes. The conveyor bridge is clad in curved steel panels with shallower ribs.

1

1   Conveyor bridge shelters main building entrance
2   Cantilevered, curved corners cover air intakes
3   Service entrance to main warehouse floor
Following pages:
    Distribution wing with truck docks and conveyor
    bridge

2

3

Estée Lauder Research Laboratories

Design/Completion (4 phases) 1983/1998
Melville, New York
Estée Lauder Companies
(Joint venture with Davis, Brody & Associates)
9000 square meters
Steel structure, concrete slabs
Steel panels, window walls

This complex is part of a campus of adjacent buildings designed by our firm (see pp. 136–143) which house manufacturing, assembly, distribution, research, and office functions for this multi-national cosmetics firm. Built over a 15-year period, the growth of this cosmetics research laboratory paralleled the growth of the company. The first phase involved the renovation of an existing, one-story building, while subsequent phases comprised several two-story additions linked to the existing structure by sky-lit, linear atrium spaces. The atriums serve as circulation, cafeteria, and informal meeting venues.

In order to visually relate this facility to adjoining company buildings, deep-rib steel panels cover the one-story building, while shallower panels with curved corners enclose the two-story additions.

1

2

144

1 Two-story-high entrance adjoins one-story wing
2 Two-story wings surround lower building section
3 Atrium entrance at "seam" between building
   sections

3

4   Atrium allows windowed offices at building
    interior
5   Main atrium is both circulation and meeting space

4

5

Hertz Orlando Airport Facility

Design/Completion 1994/1996
Orlando, Florida
The Hertz Corporation
2800 square meters (enclosed space)
6000 square meters (sheltered space)
Steel structure, concrete slabs
Steel, fiberglass panels, window walls

One of the busiest car-rental operations in the world, the Hertz Orlando Airport Facility handles one million people per year in a building complex appropriate to its exotic, tropical setting. This somewhat heroic movement of vehicles, families, and luggage takes place in a facility designed to render the process legible, transparent, and welcoming. Both indoor and outdoor areas evoke a human-made, tropical forest offering shelter from sun and rain. Undulating, petal-like, modular fiberglass canopies on metal stems protect exterior drop-off and pick-up areas, identify the facility and create a sense of comfort, safety, and welcome for the weary traveler.

Interior transactions take place in a crisp, orthogonal building of metal and glass, clearly visible from the outdoors. The ceiling repeats the forms of the exterior canopies, using wood slats in waveforms around interior columns. Other service buildings on the site—car washing, fueling, and employee amenities—utilize the same design language of rectangular volumes and waveform canopies.

1   Main building entrance with wave-form trellis
2   Section through Customer Service Building

1

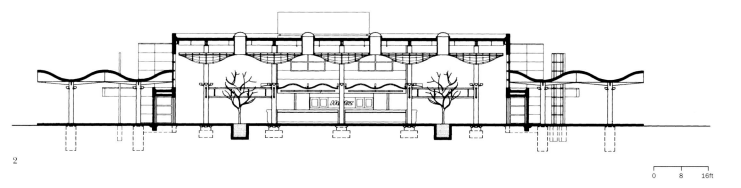

2

0 8 16ft

3

4

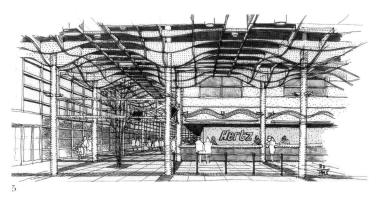

5

6

7

Estée Lauder Distribution Center

Design/Completion 1996/1998
Lachen, Switzerland
Estée Lauder Companies
(Joint Venture with Davis Brody Bond)
9000 square meters
Steel structure, rack supported roof and walls
Steel panels, window walls, glass overhangs

A rare opportunity to design a new facility adjoining a manufacturing building that was designed by our firm and completed 25 years previously. The distribution center represents the state-of-the-art in automated storage, retrieval, picking, packing, and shipping. A system of computer-guided, independent *chariots* load, transport, stack, retrieve, and deliver pallets of materials and finished products.

Designed to the highest levels of sustainable, "green" architecture, the 23-meter-high warehouse is partially below grade, with both roof and wall panels supported by the storage-rack system. Insulated wall panels and a 30-centimeter-thick sod roof, which both insulates and retains rainwater for gradual release to the local storm water system, further enhance the energy efficiency of the facility. An on-site co-generation plant provides electricity and heating for the building complex.

The building is located at the foothills of the Alps, and all office and distribution workers have views of the landscape through a sophisticated window wall which includes operable windows (air-conditioning for industrial buildings is prohibited in Switzerland), glass sun shades, and automated external blinds. A steel grid trellis and covered walkway links and visually unifies the new and former structures, while providing a security perimeter.

1

1 Window wall with operable windows and glass
  shades
2 Steel grid trellis extends past building
3 Two-story distribution wing

2

3

4   Glass shades, automated exterior blinds
5   Office areas reinforce openness and maximize
    views
6   Conveyor-supplied picking and packing level
7   Corner view reveals organization of shades and
    blinds
8   Assembly and staging level
Following pages:
    Warehouse, distribution building, and connecting
    trellis and walkway

4

5

6

7

8

Public Utilities

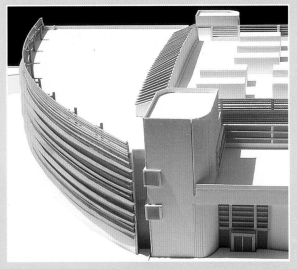

Richard Dattner & Partners Architects

Con Edison Customer Service Facility, Brooklyn

Design/Completion 1994/1997
Brooklyn, New York
Consolidated Edison Company
750 square meters
Porcelain tile, metal columns, plasterboard

Customers visit this street-level facility to make payments, ask questions, or resolve problems regarding electric services. Con Edison wanted the design to communicate respect for its customers, as well as the company's commitment to energy conservation and prudent use of resources. Energy-conserving lighting, and a clean, efficient layout facilitate circulation by customers, with staff amenities located behind a curved wall. The materials used—porcelain floor tiles, slate wall panels, and stainless steel column covers—are both environmentally benign and easy to maintain.

1

1   Slate entrance wall guides customers into facility
2   Customer service representatives are clearly visible
3   Customer service representative stations

2

3

Con Edison Gas System Control Room

Design/Completion 1993/1994
Bronx, New York
Consolidated Edison Company
930 square meters
Carpet, metal columns, glass walls

This facility controls the distribution, storage, and supply of Con Edison's gas delivery system in the Bronx. Engineers continuously monitor the condition and status of each component in this vital energy network. During emergency conditions, additional technical staff can be accommodated in the 24-hour facility. Clear sightlines, special lighting, and interior window walls facilitate communication among staff during crisis-management situations. Ergonomically designed workstation consoles integrate computers and communications to enhance staff performance and comfort.

1

1 Ergonomically designed computer/
  communication consoles
2 Clear sightlines facilitate communication during
  emergencies

2

Con Edison Customer Service Facility, The "Hub", Bronx

Design/Completion 1991/1992
Bronx, New York
Consolidated Edison Company
750 square meters
Brick, porcelain tile, security glass, plastic laminate

One block from the West 149th Street "Hub" that forms the commercial center of the South Bronx, this customer service center for Con Edison provides an important neighborhood service, collecting payments for gas end electricity from community residents. A low, modest structure, it nevertheless aims to express public accessibility, civic presence, and dignity, with a palette of simple and inexpensive materials befitting a utility attempting to educate the public to conserve energy. A simple structural system of regular bays, large window areas, bands of contrasting bricks, and a stainless steel canopy utilize ordinary materials to create a sense of welcome and familiarity. The interior is organized to make the process of seeking assistance, or paying a bill, as effortless as possible.

1

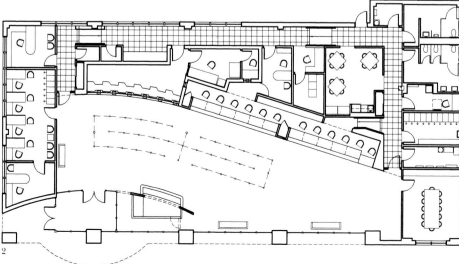

2

1   Conference room window
2   Floor plan
3   Main façade with building entrance
4   Open floor enhances visibility

3

4

Con Edison Customer Service Facility, Westchester Square, Bronx

Design/Completion 1978/1981
Bronx, New York
Consolidated Edison Company
2800 square meters
Steel frame, concrete slabs
Ground-face concrete blocks, glass block, steel

Con Edison requested "dignity on a budget"—a simple, functional design that avoids any impression of wasteful expenditure of customers' money. Located on Westchester Square, a busy urban node and commercial center, the building's two-story corner entrance matches the surrounding scale, and is both highly visible and inviting. The exterior material is polished concrete block scored into 8-inch squares and accented by two lines of glazed orange brick. Large glass panels enclose the two-story lobby.

Consistent with Con Edison's message of energy conservation, south-facing, upper-level windows are shielded from summer sun by an aluminum sunscreen, while first-floor windows are set back under a protective overhang. Windows on the north wall are set flush with the wall surface.

1   Two-story corner entrance
2   Customer service counter
3   Entrance lobby with information counter

1

2

3

Sherman Creek State Park

Design 1972
Manhattan, New York
New York State Office of Parks, Recreation & Historic Preservation
Consolidated Edison Company
18,600 square meters
Steel frame, concrete slabs

The Consolidated Edison Sherman Creek Generating Station, built in 1908 to serve upper Manhattan, was closed in 1970 because its coal-burning boilers could not meet air standards. A study commissioned by New York State Parks found that the plant structure and enclosed spaces were well suited for conversion to an urban recreation center. The large spans and high ceilings could accommodate a wide variety of activities: a bowling alley, indoor skating rink, experimental theater, gymnasium, and roof deck. The former coal-storage bunkers were convertible into a swimming pool, and the former loading tower could become an observation deck and snack bar. A new marina and waterfront promenade would link the restored generating plant to the surrounding community.

The economic recession of 1975 and the growing awareness of the hazards of asbestos caused this project to be abandoned. Three years later, New York State decided to locate its new park on the roof of the North River Pollution Treatment Facility. That project, Riverbank State Park, was realized, and is described on pages 76–81. The concept of re-using a generating plant as a recreation resource remains an intriguing possibility.

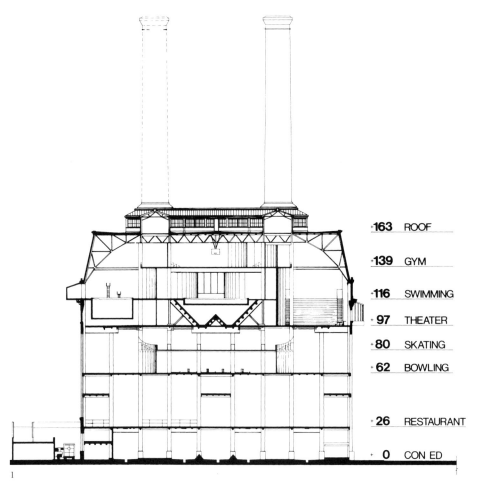

+163	ROOF
+139	GYM
+116	SWIMMING
+97	THEATER
+80	SKATING
+62	BOWLING
+26	RESTAURANT
+0	CON ED

1

2

1 Cross-section through generating plant
2 The Sherman Creek Generating Plant in 1970
3 Gymnasium within former coal conveyor level
4 Restored plant generates recreation
5 Site plan of State Park and new residential
   community

170

3

4

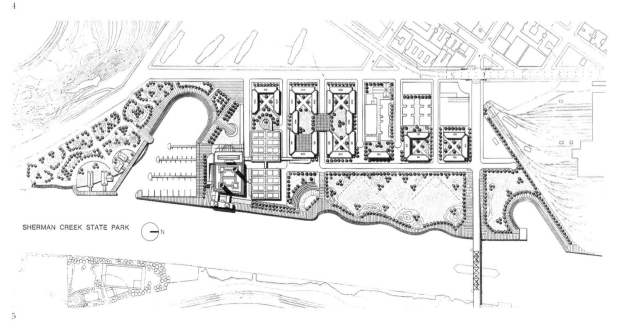

SHERMAN CREEK STATE PARK

5

Con Edison Service Building

Design/Completion 1998/2001
New York, New York
Consolidated Edison Company
9050 square meters
Steel frame, concrete slabs
Ground-face concrete blocks, glass curtain wall

Con Edison commissioned this three-story office, warehouse, and "work-out" building for a site at East 16th Street and East River Drive, adjoining their vast steam-generating plant. Designed to utilize, and demonstrate, contemporary strategies for energy conservation and sustainability, the building will house technicians and equipment for servicing Con Ed's steam, gas, and electric distribution systems throughout the city.

The ground floor is a storage facility for tools, spare parts, and other materials required for routine and emergency repairs. The second floor houses the various operating departments—steam, electric, gas etc.—with muster rooms and locker facilities. The third floor is a flexible office floor for engineering and technical support staff. A sophisticated, curved curtain wall maximizes daylight while limiting direct sunlight into the facility. The central skylight on the third level brings additional daylight deep into the building.

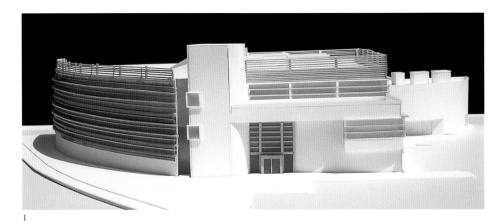

1

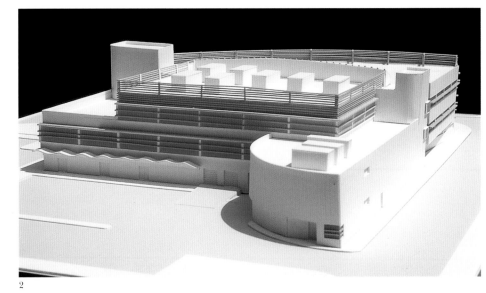

2

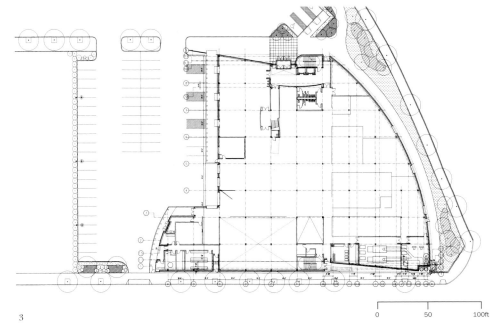

3

0   50   100ft

1 East 16th Street main entrance
2 View of building and service yard
3 Plan of first floor and service yard
4 Aerial view shows central skylight
5 Sketch of main entrance
Following pages:
   Service Building, with generating plant beyond

4

5

Civic Infrastructure

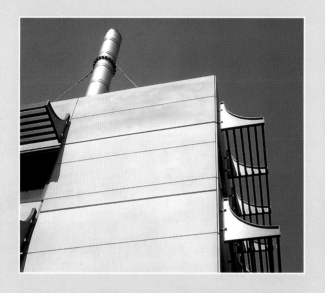

Richard Dattner & Partners Architects

Marine Transfer Station, W. 59th Street

Design/Completion 1984/1987
New York, New York
New York City Department of Sanitation/
Greeley & Hansen Engineers
5500 square meters
Steel structure, concrete slabs
Steel, concrete, metal and fiberglass panels

The 13,000 tons of solid waste accumulating daily in New York City are collected by sanitation trucks and brought to a series of Marine Transfer Stations (MTS) along the city's shoreline. This MTS is located in one of two facilities on the Hudson River designed by our firm. The trucks drive up an enclosed ramp to an upper-level tipping floor, where the trucks back up and "tip" their loads into open barges waiting below. The filled barges, formerly dumped in the Atlantic, are currently towed by tugs to a vast sanitary landfill on Staten Island. This landfill will shortly reach capacity, and the barges will be towed to alternate locations.

This building replaced a 19th-century MTS whose historic façade was reconstructed as the entrance gateway to the new facility. In keeping with the industrial vernacular of the New York waterfront, the exposed steel structure is clad in metal panels, with large areas of translucent fiberglass window walls for natural lighting. At night neon lights by artist Steven Antonakos outline the primary façade and a row of windows facing north—creating a landmark for motorists entering Midtown.

1

2

1 Recreated historic façade becomes new entrance
gateway
2 Exposed steel internal structure
3 View from Hudson River shore
4 Garbage barge bay below "tipping floor"

3

4

5

Brooklyn District Garages 1 & 4

Design/Completion 1997/2001
Brooklyn, New York, USA
New York City Department of Sanitation
11,000 square meters
Steel structure, concrete slabs
Steel, concrete, brick, metal panels

The sanitation trucks that pick up New York City's solid waste, plow snow, and salt the streets are stored, fueled, and repaired in District Garages serving specific geographic areas. This facility comprises two distinct garages built along a common service drive. Sanitation vehicles drive down this service road to rear entrances for both garages—where they are fueled, washed, and prepared for the next day's run. A series of overhead doors along the front building façade provide for the efficient dispatch of large numbers of vehicles. Trucks requiring repair are serviced in bays along the common drive.

The independent garages have curved, mirror-image façades, and are visually unified by the Brooklyn District Office bridging between the two buildings. This curved form is canted forward slightly, crowning the linked buildings, creating a monumental scale, and defining the entrance to the complex. The undulations of the flanking façades are continued in the wave-shaped, glazed canopies over the front doors.

1

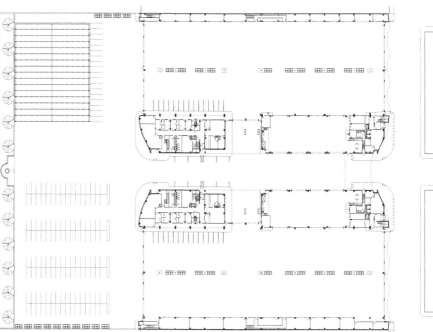

2

1 Brooklyn District Office forms a bridge between
  garages
2 Plan of main level
3 Pedestrian view of front façade

3

33rd Police Precinct House

Design/Completion 1995/2000
New York, New York
New York City Police Department
New York City Department of Design & Construction
9000 square meters
Steel structure, concrete slabs
Steel, concrete, brick, metal roof

New York City's community policing initiative has transformed the relationship between the Police Department and the neighborhoods its officers protect, and is now a model for other police departments. To the traditional role of protecting the community and fighting crime, the police have added preventive measures, education, and outreach. Familiarity with the neighborhood helps the police gain the trust of the community, identify potential problems, and reduce criminal behavior. The new 33rd Police Precinct House reflects the duality of these roles by creating a "friendly fortress".

A long, circular brick façade wrapping around two sides of the building recalls some of New York's historic fortresses. Slicing through this curve is an internal street, with the public entrance facing a small plaza and the police entrance from an enclosed parking yard. Glazed at both entrances, and covered by a soaring curved roof and linear clerestory, this atrium opens the building to the community, invites public access, and reveals some of the activities housed in the building. Locker rooms, communications centers, and other functions requiring privacy are located in the cellar and on the upper level.

1

2

184

1   View from the north along Amsterdam Avenue
2   Model view of public entrance to atrium
3   Model view of curved façade and internal street

3

New York City Police Academy

Design 1992
Bronx, New York
New York City Police Department
New York City Department of Design & Construction
22,000 square meters
Steel structure, concrete slabs
Steel, concrete, brick, metal roof

The runner-up in an invited competition, this design represents a balance between police and community, respecting the low scale of the Grand Concourse neighborhood and providing community access to the playing field/parade ground, while creating a clear distinction between the building's functional sections. The building is an open, permeable fortress, recalling familiar historic precedents such as armories, urban college campuses, and parade grounds. Expressive of its civic importance, it "fits in" to the urban fabric of the Bronx's "Champs Elysee".

A round entrance tower organizes entrances for the public, recruits, in-service personnel, and staff along three axes. The public follows the central axis into the parade ground, or to the auditorium, lecture room, and Police Museum in the round tower. A rooftop observation platform, topped by a communications mast, satellite dishes, and antennas provides a scenic overlook and neighborhood landmark. Parking, storage, receiving, and firing ranges are located on lower levels, raising the open field to the level of the surrounding streets.

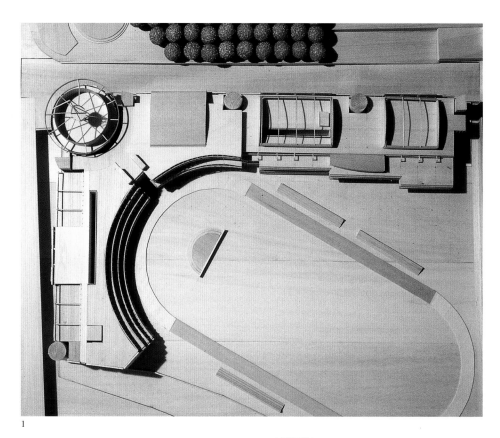

1

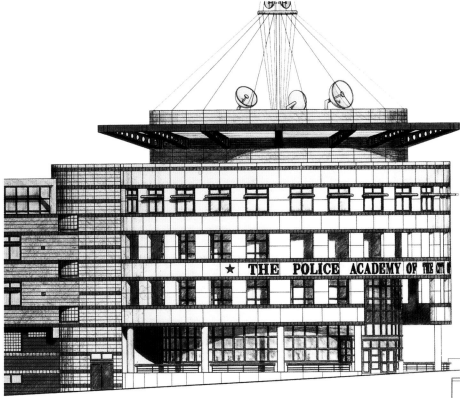

2

1 Aerial view of model
2 Round entrance tower and observation level
3 West elevation
4 Model view from the Grand Concourse
5 Main entrance and plaza

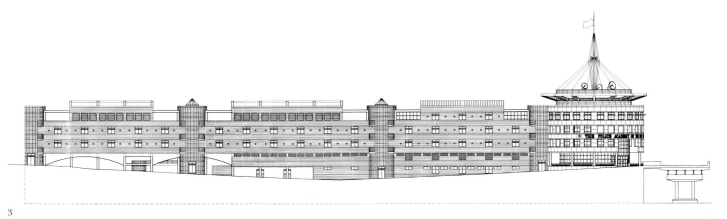

3

4

5

Engine Company 75, Ladder Company 33, Battalion 19

Design/Completion 1997/2000
Bronx, New York
New York City Fire Department
New York City Department of Design & Construction
P.M.S. Construction Corp.
Steel structure, concrete slabs
Steel, concrete, concrete blocks, glass blocks

Two Fire Department Companies and a Battalion Chief share the first new firehouse built in New York City in 15 years. Sited on a corner in a residential neighborhood, the new building uses striated, contrasting concrete blocks to express an essential civic function while respecting the scale of the surrounding neighborhood. A corner tower recalls the fire observation towers once used in protecting New York.

The single-story apparatus floor at the street intersection allows fire vehicles to exit to four directions. An "L" shaped, two-story building section surrounds the apparatus floor, housing dormitories for fire personnel on the upper level, and battalion offices, dining room, and kitchen on the lower level. On the east façade of the firehouse, artist Mierle Ukeles has outlined a full-size ladder truck in concrete and glass blocks.

1

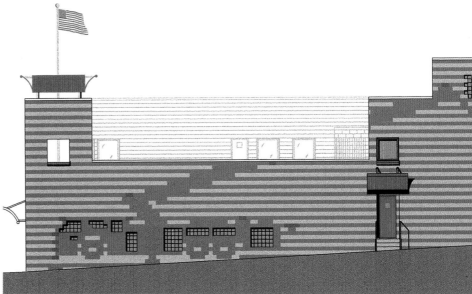

2

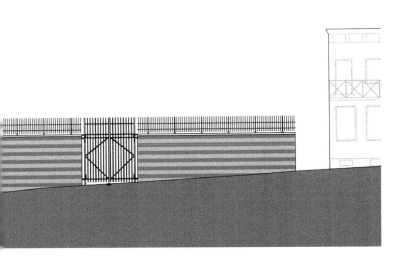

1 Model view of apparatus doors and fire tower
2 East façade with ladder truck outline
3 Plan of apparatus level

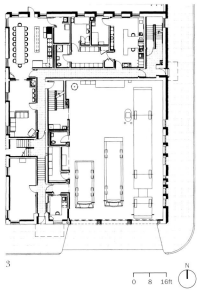

3

0 8 16ft

N

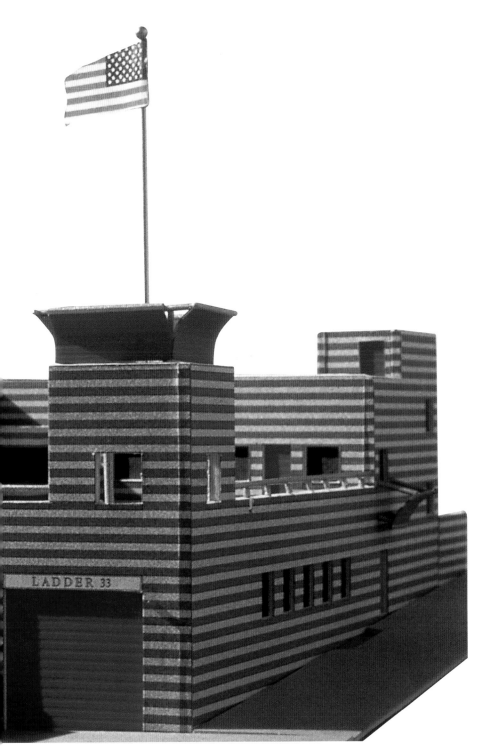

26th Ward Sludge Treatment Facility

Design/completion 1989/1996
Brooklyn, New York
New York City Department of Environmental Protection
Stone & Webster/Hazen & Sawyer, Engineers
18,000 square meters
Steel structure, concrete slabs
Steel, precast concrete, window walls, glass

Sludge is the semi-solid residue of the sewage treatment process. Until 1988, when the U.S. Congress banned ocean dumping, the sludge from New York City's sewerage plants was dumped in the Atlantic Ocean, about 100 miles from the city. Turning this liquid waste into a material that could be handled and disposed of on land ultimately involved the construction of sludge dewatering and storage facilities at eight of the City's 14 water pollution control plants. Built at a cost of $545 million in only 42 months, these structures were treating all of the City's sludge by June of 1992.

In order to accomplish this extensive construction program quickly and cost-effectively, a "kit-of-parts" was developed, consisting of precast concrete panels, aluminum cornice/sun-shade units, modular window walls, pyramid skylights around the plant stacks, earth berms, and indigenous planting. These standard building elements link the facilities visually, while allowing for varying combinations and colors of elements to reflect the local requirements of each site.

1

1 Sludge storage (foreground) and dewatering
  facilities
2 Aluminum louvres form cornices and window
  shades
3 Map of sludge treatment facility locations
4 "Kit-of-parts"
Following pages:
  Window wall reveals sludge centrifuges inside
  plant

2

3

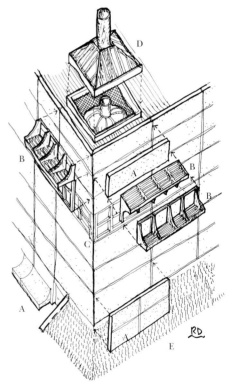

4

A Precast concrete panels
B Aluminum cornice/sun-shade
  units
C Modular window walls
D Pyramid skylights
E Earth berms

Bowery Bay Sewage Treatment Facility

Design/Completion 1984/2001
Queens, New York
New York City Department of Environmental Protection
Hazen & Sawyer/Stone & Webster, Engineers
12,000 square meters
Steel structure, concrete slabs
Steel, precast concrete, window walls, glass

The Bowery Bay Sewage Treatment Facility, like most of New York City's sewage treatment facilities, was built during the Works Progress Administration (WPA) in the 1930s—its monumental architecture and bas-relief sculptures expressing the heroism of labor and public works. These designs for the new sludge dewatering facility, expansion of the pump house, and new screening building continue the architectural language of the original buildings, while differentiating new buildings from the original structures. Horizontal banding unifies the five new buildings and introduces a human scale to these large structures.

1

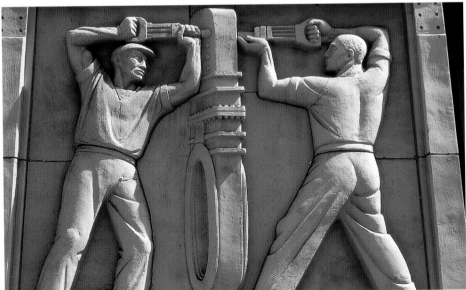

2

194

1 New sludge dewatering facility
2 The heroism of labor and public works
3 Elevation of pump house expansion
4 Master plan of modernized plant
5 South elevation preserving the original main
  entrance

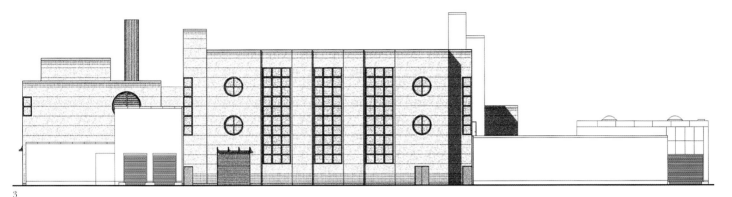

3

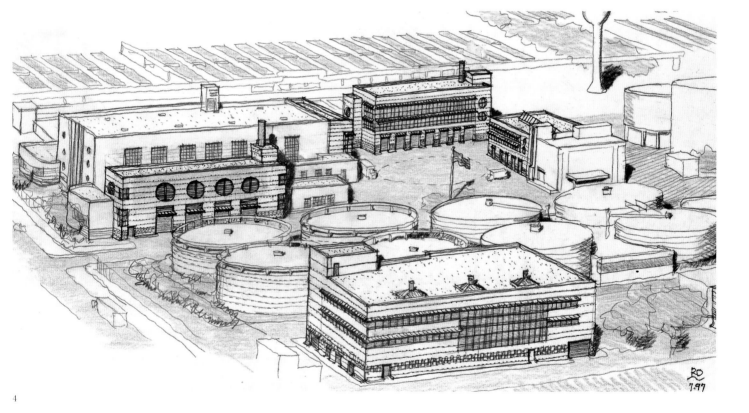

4

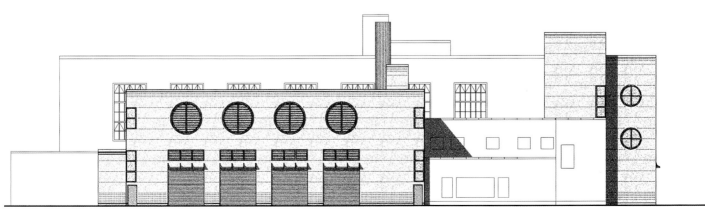

5

Wards Island Sludge Treatment Facility

Design/Completion 1989/1995
Manhattan, New York
New York City Department of Environmental Protection
Stone & Webster/Hazen & Sawyer, Engineers
18,000 square meters
Steel structure, concrete slabs
Steel, precast concrete, window walls, glass

The process of dewatering sludge involves large centrifuges that spin the sludge—removing most of the liquid and yielding a smaller volume of "sludge cake". Window walls allow views into the dewatering facility, illustrate this benign process, and allay possible community concerns.

In keeping with the somewhat classical architectural treatment of the original Wards Island sewage treatment plant, the aluminum louvres are here used as a decorative cornice—capping the buildings and casting shadows which enliven the concrete façades.

1

2

1 End elevation of sludge storage building
2 Side elevation expresses sludge storage bins within
3 Aluminium louvre cornices
4 Window wall reveals interior process equipment

3

4

Tallman Island Sludge Treatment Facility

Design/Completion 1989/ 1992
Queens, New York
New York City Department of Environmental Protection
Stone & Webster/Hazen & Sawyer Engineers
4800 square meters
Steel structure, concrete slabs
Steel, precast concrete, window walls, glass

The sludge dewatering facility prototypes
were designed in two prototypical sizes,
and the Tallman Island facility is one of
the smaller versions. Built at a shorefront
site, the extensive window walls allow views
through the building interior to the bay
beyond. Settling tanks around the building
become reflecting pools.

1

1 Sludge dewatering building and settling tanks
2 Window wall reveals internal process equipment
3 View from East River

2

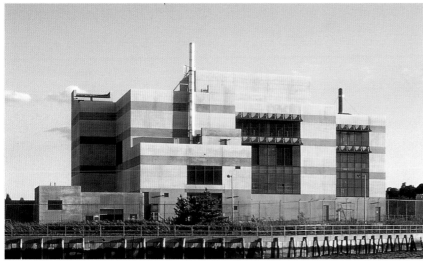

3

Oakwood Beach Sludge Treatment Facility

Design/Completion 1989/1992
Staten Island, New York
New York City Department of Environmental Protection
Stone & Webster/Hazen & Sawyer, Engineers
9000 square meters
Steel structure, concrete slabs
Steel, precast concrete, window walls, glass

The Gateway National Recreation Area surrounds the Oakwood Beach Sewage Treatment Plant, and the sludge facility is visible across an area of wetlands and sand dunes adjoining a community of former summer bungalows converted into year-round homes. Precast concrete panels, in alternating bands of off-white and warm gray, unify the four structures (two buildings, a circular tank, and a tower) into a slightly surrealist and oddly festive composition. Seen from the distant seashore they resemble over-scaled beach cabanas lost among the dunes.

1

2

1 Dewatering facility and tower
2 Dewatering and sludge storage buildings
3 Window wall with aluminum sunshades

3

Amtrak/Long Island Railroad Ventilation Structures

Design/Completion 1997/2001
Manhattan and Queens, New York
Amtrak/Long Island Railroad
Parsons, Brinckerhoff, Quade and Douglas
3600 square meters, 50 meters deep
Concrete structure
Concrete, brick, stainless steel louvres, glass bricks

Four tunnels connect Manhattan's Pennsylvania Station to Queens, Long Island, and New England. Serving both Amtrak and the Long Island Railroad since the early 1900s, the tunnels now require upgraded ventilation, and emergency access and exit capability. The Manhattan site is on First Avenue, adjoining the New York University Medical Center. Designs for this site integrate the functional requirements of the ventilation shafts with the planned expansion of the Medical Center.

The Long Island City shaft structure allows future Queens West commercial development over and around the new building. The structure is designed to function both as a freestanding building, and as part of the future development. A band of stainless steel louvres provides for air intake, or exhaust for the reversible fans within the structure.

1

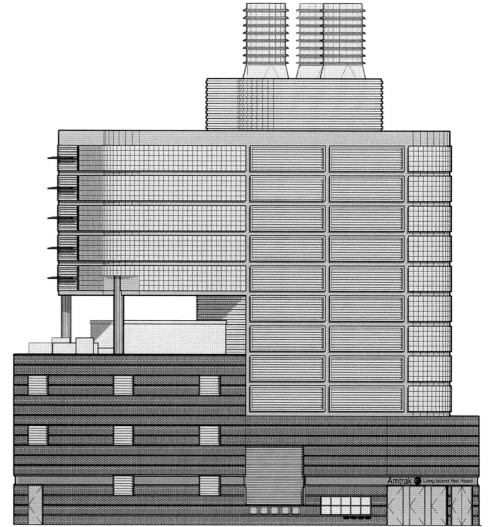

1 Ventilation structure at First Avenue
2 First Avenue elevation
3 Section at railroad tunnel under East River
4 Long Island City ventilation structure
5 Plan of railroad tunnels

2

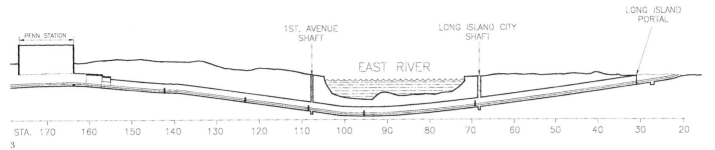

3

PENN STATION

1ST. AVENUE SHAFT

LONG ISLAND CITY SHAFT

LONG ISLAND PORTAL

EAST RIVER

STA. 170 160 150 140 130 120 110 100 90 80 70 60 50 40 30 20

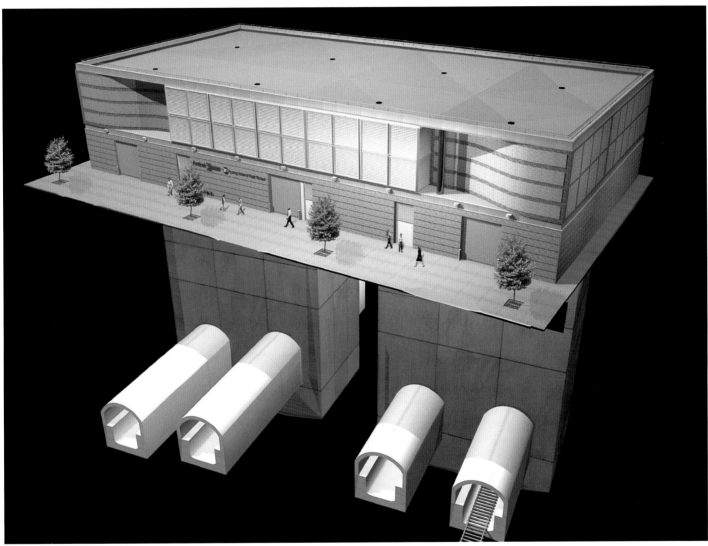

4

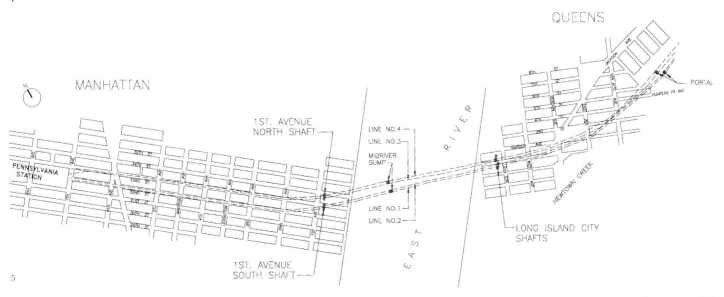

5

QUEENS

MANHATTAN

1ST. AVENUE NORTH SHAFT

LINE NO.4
LINE NO.3
MIDRIVER SUMP

LINE NO.1
LINE NO.2

PENNSYLVANIA STATION

EAST RIVER

PORTAL

HUNTERS PT AVE

NEWTOWN CREEK

LONG ISLAND CITY SHAFTS

1ST. AVENUE SOUTH SHAFT

Paerdegat Basin Combined Sewage Overflow Facility

Design/Completion 1997/2002
Brooklyn, New York
New York City Department of Environmental Protection
Hazen & Sawyer Engineers
10,000 square meters
Steel structure, concrete tanks and deck
Steel, concrete, metal roofing, masonry

During periods of heavy rainfall, the volume of New York City's combined storm and sanitary sewers exceeds the capacity of the sewage treatment plants—the resulting "overflow" drains into the City's waterways untreated. A series of Combined Sewage Overflow (CSO) facilities are being built to store the overflow in huge concrete tanks until the sewage can be pumped to nearby treatment facilities.

The Paerdegat facility is located along Paerdegat Basin—a channel originally dredged to permit shipping, and which has become the site of boating clubs and a natural resource education area. The sewage storage tanks are below grade—under a landscaped plaza and riverfront promenade. Above-grade structures are enclosed under curved, overhanging metal roofs to minimize the visual impact of these large structures. The existing pump house will be restored as part of the new development.

1 Aerial view of site model
2 Model with Paedegat Basin in foreground
3 New screening and service buildings

1

2

3

Catskill-Delaware Filtration Facility

Design 1995/2000
Westchester County, New York State
New York City Department of Environmental Protection
Hazen & Sawyer/Camp Dresser & McKee
54,000 square meters
Concrete tanks, steel roof structure
Concrete, steel, masonry, metal roofing

The Catskill-Delaware watershed provides much of New York City's water supply—currently at sufficient purity to require no filtration. Population growth and development in the watershed may eventually compromise water quality, and therefore the City is under a Federal mandate to prepare a master plan for future filtration and purification of the Catskill-Delaware water supply.

Located above the existing aqueduct system on a suburban site, this preliminary design creates a campus of low, horizontal structures organized around a central water channel and fountains. The required large tanks are mostly below grade, to reduce the scale of the above-grade buildings. Curved roofs, striated masonry walls, and extensive landscaping help integrate this campus into its natural setting. If this filtration plant is ultimately built, it will represent one of the largest public works projects ever realized in New York City.

1

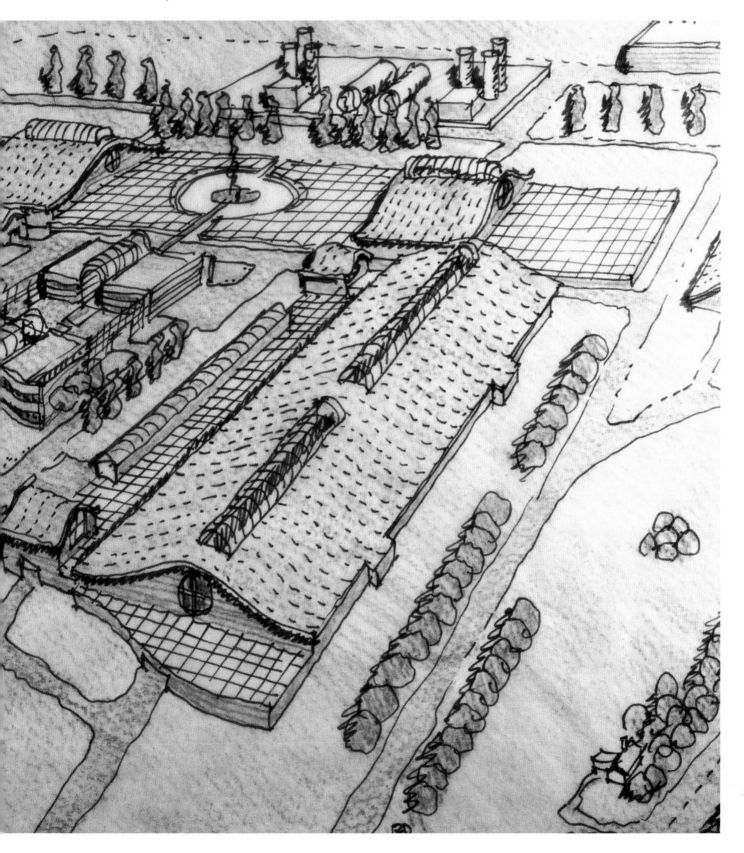

Transportation/Transit

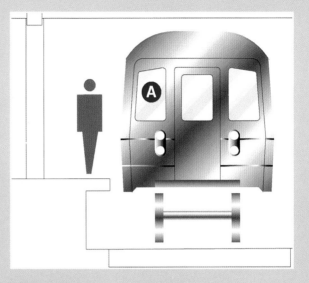

Richard Dattner & Partners Architects

Newark International Airport Vertical Transportation

Design/Completion 1999/2000
Newark International Airport, New Jersey
Port Authority of New York & New Jersey
Steel structure
Steel, laminated glass, hydraulic elevators

New York City's fastest-growing airport commissioned a variety of interventions to facilitate passenger flow while respecting the architecture of the existing terminals. Exterior modifications include fiberglass canopies marking terminal entries, and way-finding graphics.

Glass-enclosed elevators, relocated escalators, and new parking-level vestibules and ground transportation areas facilitate access to the arrivals, concourse and departures levels for travelers with baggage carts. The elevator cores are freestanding, glazed shafts that enhance visibility and security, and provide a crisp, contemporary counterpoint to the concrete terminal structure.

The project involves significant structural modifications as well as careful staging to minimize impacts and maintain terminal operations during construction. When completed, the airport redevelopment plan will create new arrivals and departures levels to accommodate increased passenger traffic.

1

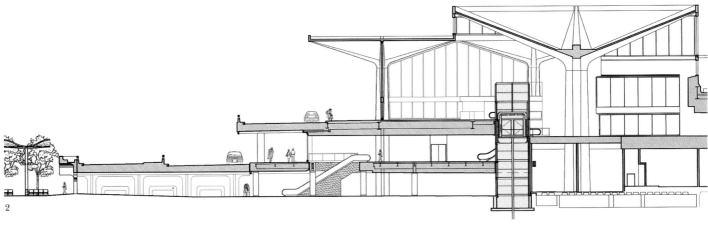

2

1   New entrance canopies
2   Section at new elevators and vestibule
3   Computer view of elevator enclosure

3

JFK International Airport International Arrivals Building Renewal Project

Design/Completion 1994/1995
JFK International Airport, New York
Port Authority of New York & New Jersey
4,000 square meters
aluminum ceilings, lighting, graphics

As the first phase of a comprehensive redevelopment of New York City's largest airport, the International Arrivals Building was upgraded and revitalized. Working with lighting designer Domingo Gonzalez and graphic designer Louis Nelson, a series of long, gloomy corridors are transformed using new ceilings, lighting, wall murals and the Port Authority's significant art collection.

An open-grid ceiling and new directional signage renew the concourse corridors. Two art galleries are created in the mezzanines that formerly overlooked the customs zone. The service and immigration corridors contain quotations from the Bill of Rights and flag murals to create a calming, dignified and uplifting entry for arriving overseas passengers.

1

2

1 New arrival and immigration corridor
2 Departure concourse level
3 International Arrivals Building Art Gallery

3

42nd Street 8th Avenue Station
Port Authority Bus Terminal

Design/Completion 1998/2002
New York City, New York
MTA New York City Transit (Joint venture with Parsons Brinckerhoff)
350 meters long
Steel structure, concrete slabs
Steel, concrete, tile, granite pavers

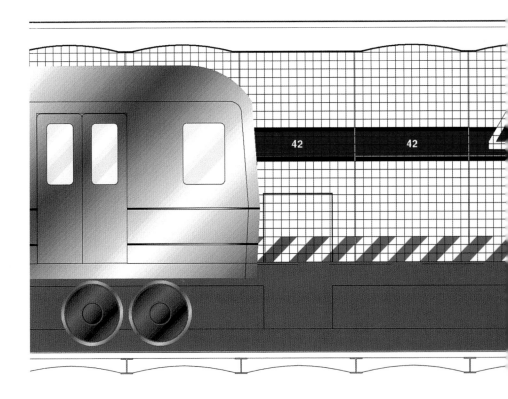

One of New York City's busiest subway stations, this facility is a gateway to the city for thousands of passengers arriving from the adjacent Port Authority Bus Terminal, as well as from the western anchor for the transformed 42nd Street, extending one block east to Times Square. Extending for four blocks under 8th Avenue, the station is also one of the longest in the transit system.

The platform level will receive new granite pavers, lighting, signage, and tiled panels along the platform walls. The station's sign identifying it as "42" will be integrated into new station graphics consistent with station standards for the IND line.

A mezzanine-level shopping concourse will be revitalized with illuminated advertising and cultural event panels, additional commercial space, a setting for musical performances, and a major public art installation.

1

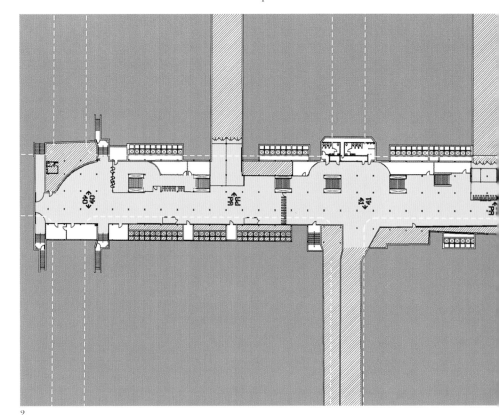

2

3

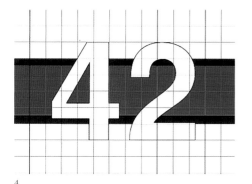

1 MTA Transit Subway Map
2 Plan of mezzanine level
3 Section/elevation of new track walls
4 Station identification on track walls

4

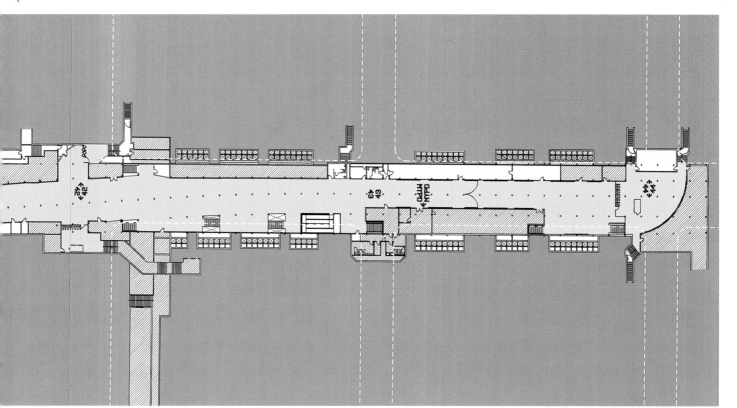

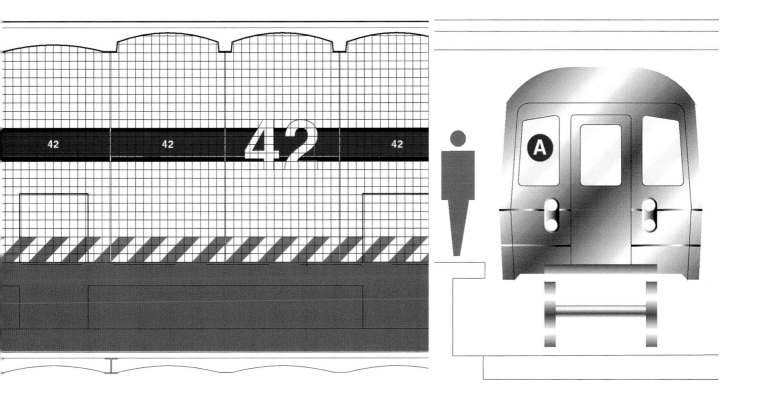

Queensboro Plaza Station

Design/Completion 1994/2000
Queens, New York
MTA New York City Transit
160 meters long
Steel structure, concrete slabs
Steel, concrete, tile

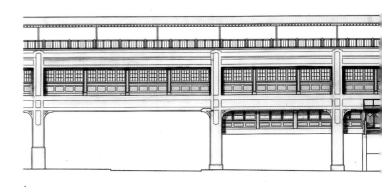

1

Situated at the eastern terminus of the Queensboro Bridge, this elevated station is a major transit gateway and significant architectural landmark. Originally twice the width, with double the number of tracks, the station had its northern half removed in 1960—leaving the original concrete structure on the south elevation and an exposed steel structure on the north.

The design emphasizes the unique aspects of each elevation—with the restoration of the original, decorative concrete elements and windows of the historic façade, and the introduction of a new curtain wall on the truncated façade. The distinctive linear canopy at the upper platform level is restored, and replicas of the original bench and station identification partitions are installed along this level. Raised pedestrian overpasses are covered by a similar metal canopy.

2

3

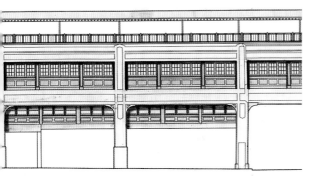

1 South elevation
2 Computer model of elevated station
3 Mezzanine control level
4 Upper platform level
5 MTA Transit subway map

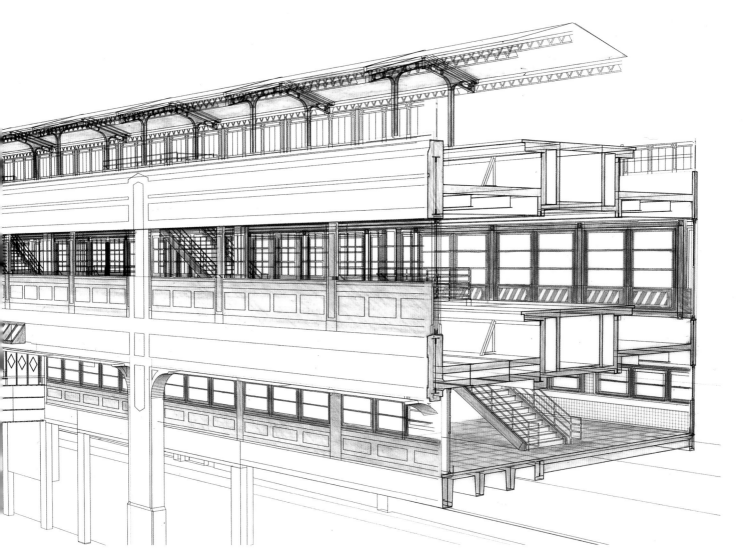

5

Pelham Parkway Station

Design/Completion 1998/2002
Bronx, New York
MTA New York City Transit (Joint venture with Parsons Brinckerhoff)
160 meters long
Steel structure, concrete slabs
Steel, concrete, tile

Built in 1917, this landmark elevated station promoted the development of the surrounding community as an early garden suburb within city limits. Pelham Parkway—a roadway within a linear park— passes under the steel-and-concrete arches supporting the station. The current redesign provides elevator access from the sidewalk to the control mezzanine, and from the mezzanine to both south and north-bound platforms.

The new elevator enclosures preserve the original architectural vocabulary, and the original structure, platform canopies, and windows are restored or repaired. Sidewalk widening at the corners under the station entrances improves both vehicular and pedestrian flow at this busy intersection.

1

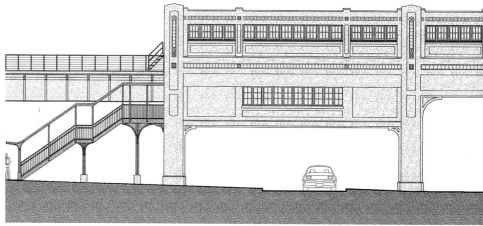

2

1   Elevation at elevator tower
2   West elevation of elevated station
3   Section at elevator tower
4   MTA Transit subway map

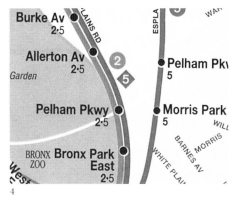

4

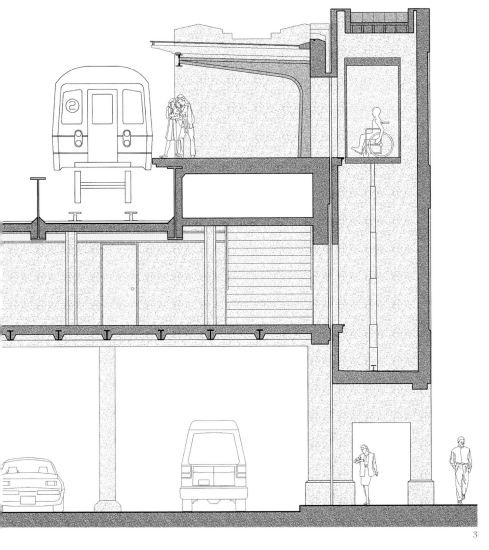

3

72nd Street Station, Broadway

Design/Completion 1996/2003
New York City, New York
MTA New York City Transit (Joint venture with Gruzen Samton)
180 meters long
Steel structure, concrete slabs
Steel, concrete, tile, granite pavers

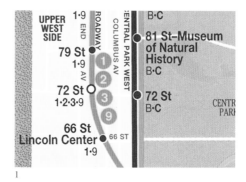

The station is located at the intersection of Broadway, Amsterdam Avenue, and West 72nd Street, and is entered through one of only three remaining free-standing station houses in New York. This historic station has been overcrowded almost since its opening in 1904. The extension of the station platforms and the re-configuration of north-bound Broadway allow for a new entrance and better use of the platform areas.

The landmark Verdi Square Park is extended to the west, creating a new public plaza at this gateway to the Upper West Side. A new station house on this plaza—a contemporary version of the original building—eases pedestrian congestion by providing multiple entrances for passengers from north of West 72nd Street. An exposed steel and glass structure creates a highly visible, secure entrance, with four additional stairways and elevator access to both uptown and downtown platforms.

The original station house is restored, and the original glass roof rebuilt. Under the Arts for Transit program, the glazed roof of the new structure is a glass-mosaic art work.

1   MTA Transit subway map
2   New Verdi Square Plaza from the south
3   View looking north from West 72nd Street
4   Section at new Station House

3

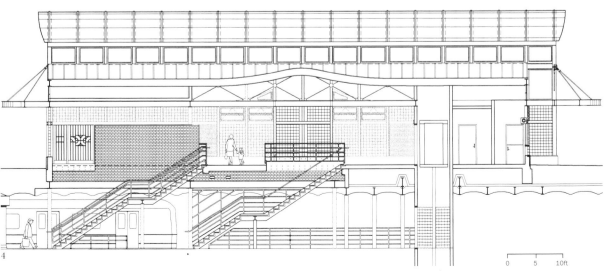

4

5

6

7

8

Modular Environments

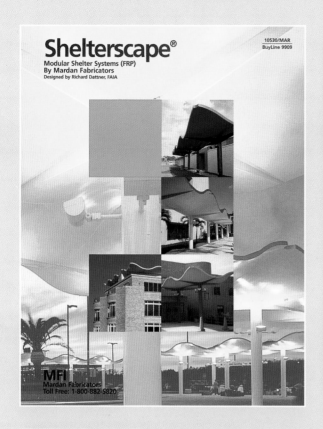

Shelterscape®
Modular Shelter Systems (FRP)
By Mardan Fabricators
Designed by Richard Dattner, FAIA

10530/MAR
BuyLine 9909

MFI
Mardan Fabricators
Toll Free: 1-800-882-5820

Streetscape®
A Modular Shelter System
Designed by Richard Dattner AIA

Northern Plastics Corporation 13.16/No.
6733 Myers Road
East Syracuse, N. Y. 13057
(315) 463 1431

Kemper Arena, Kansas City, Mo

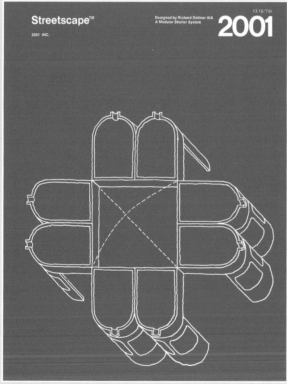

Streetscape™
2001 INC.

Designed by Richard Dattner AIA
A Modular Shelter System

13.16/TW

2001

PlayCubes™
2001 INC.

The Instant Playground

2.15/TW

2001

Richard Dattner & Partners Architects

Shelterscape Modular Shelter System

Design/Fabrication 1995/1996
Various locations in the U.S.
Richard Dattner/Mardan Fabricators, Inc.
Fiberglass-reinforced polyester panels
Steel pipe columns and splines

The Shelterscape Modular Shelter System
is based on a patented modular unit
measuring 3m x 3m (10' x 10'), which has
two straight edges and two curved edges.
This basic module can be combined in
several configurations to produce
continuous shelter—with either straight
or undulating edge profiles. Four units are
normally clustered around a tubular steel
support column anchored to a concrete
foundation. Drainage is through the
column, with internal conduits for lighting
and communication wiring. The fiberglass
units are laminated in multiple layers over
a balsa core, and the edge flanges are
further reinforced. The resulting
fabrications are rigid units capable
of withstanding 120 mile per hour
(190km/hr) winds.

Architects and engineers use the
Shelterscape system in a wide variety
of settings and applications, including
airports, transit shelters, car rental and
parking shelters, movie theater entrances,
and school bus drop-off areas. The units
have been installed adjoining buildings,
as well as supported from buildings and
on their roofs.

1

1 Steel splines support four modular units per
  column
2 Linked units shelter a bus drop-off area
3 Exploded axonometric illustrates assembly
4 Elevation of typical four-unit cluster
Following pages:
  Linked units with internal drains and lighting
  conduits

2

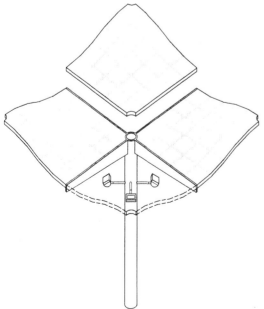

3

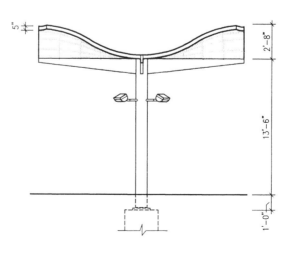

4

Customer Loading Area

Intermodal Transfer Shelters

Design 1996
New York, New York
MTA New York City Transit
Parsons Brinckerhoff Quade & Douglas
Modular units, various sizes
Steel support structure, fiberglass-reinforced polyester panels roof units

At the terminations of several New York City subway lines, passengers require "intermodal" transfers between train and surface bus routes. The commissioned design is a modular system appropriate for various locations throughout the city. Design requirements include flexibility, shelter from rain and sun, transparency (to avoid blocking views of nearby stores or creating hidden areas), security lighting, roof drainage, and provision of way-finding graphics.

The basic unit is 10' x 15' (3m x 4.5m), and can be installed in any length appropriate to each location. Multiple rows of shelters can be joined to cover large areas. Drainage is routed through the support pipes—which also contain conduits for electrical and communication wiring.

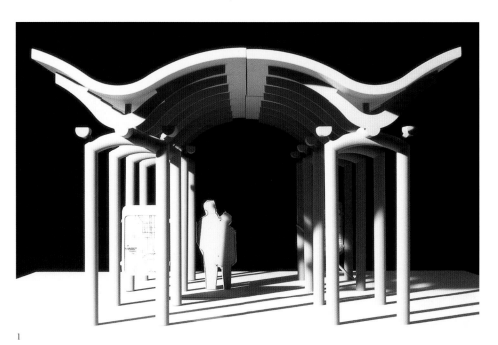

1

2

1 Two rows of shelters combined to cover a larger
   area
2 Typical linear arrangement of intermodal shelters
3 Units shelter bus entry and display system maps
4 Front elevation of basic unit
5 Side elevation shows lighting and information
   panel

3

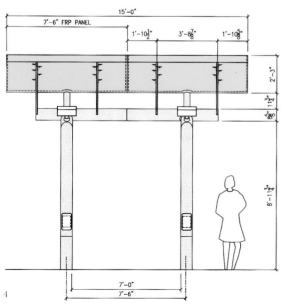

4

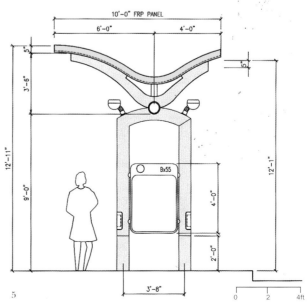

5

Streetscape Modular System

Design 1978
Various locations in the U.S. and Canada
Richard Dattner/2001 Incorporated
Modular units, various sizes
Fiberglass-reinforced polyester roof and wall panels, Lexan windows

This design was the first modular booth system widely used by architects to provide enclosures that would also complement their buildings. The modular system is both simple and flexible—consisting of curved and straight, molded fiberglass-reinforced polyester roof and wall panel units in standardized dimensions. The basic unit is a 5' (1.5m) diameter cylinder, 8' (2.4m) high. Additional wall and roof panels can be added to create almost limitless combinations.

Major Streetscape installations include Disney World, Sesame Place, O'Hare International Airport, and the 1982 World's Fair. The patented design was licensed to several manufacturers, and is now fabricated in many versions and materials.

1

2

1 Ticket booths at Kemper Arena
2 Hertz booth illustrates the most used Streetscape configuration
3 Basic building blocks of the modular system
4 Exploded isometric illustrates components
5 Axonometric of possible arrangement
6 Ticket booths at 1982 World's Fair

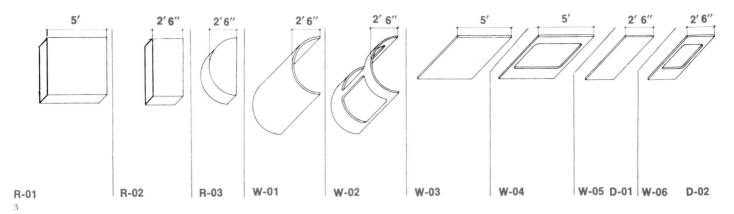

R-01   R-02   R-03   W-01   W-02   W-03   W-04   W-05 D-01 W-06   D-02

3

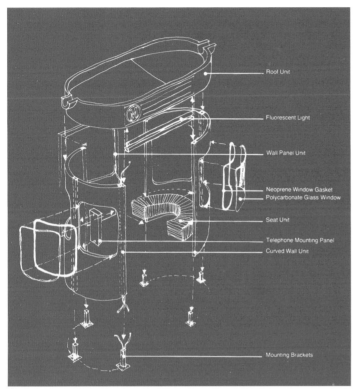

Roof Unit

Fluorescent Light

Wall Panel Unit

Neoprene Window Gasket
Polycarbonate Glass Window

Seat Unit

Telephone Mounting Panel
Curved Wall Unit

Mounting Brackets

4

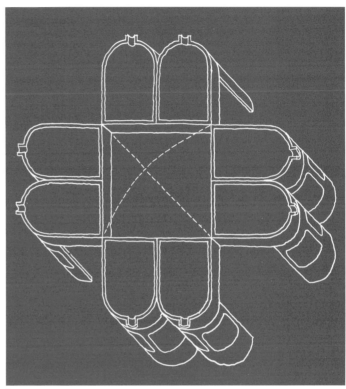

5

6

Modular House

Design/Completion 1969/1970
Amagansett, New York
Private residence
140 square meters
Stressed-skin plywood panels
Plywood, wood infill, windows

A patented system designed to provide great flexibility, ease of erection, and efficient use of materials. The basic structural unit is an "L"-shaped, stressed-skin, insulated plywood panel in two lengths—7'–6", and 12' (2.5m and 3.5m). Twelve panels are assembled into a rigid frame—measuring 16' x 16' (5m x 5m)— from which the house is constructed. These frames can be joined horizontally and stacked vertically up to three floors high. This basic geometry can be realized in concrete or steel, as well as plywood.

Once the basic structure is erected, a variety of infill wall panels, sliding glass doors, and window walls are used to enclose the house. The house illustrated here utilizes six frames to enclose 1500 square feet (140 sqm), and was erected within a few days. Sloping roof sections, skylights, and curved terrace extensions add living space and enliven its appearance.

1   Three frames with three infill options
2   Pile supported version can be built over water
3   Sloping roofs enclose a sleeping loft
4   Patent drawings of modular system

1

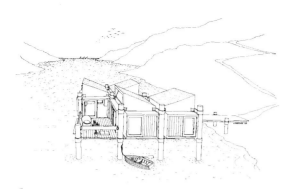

2

3

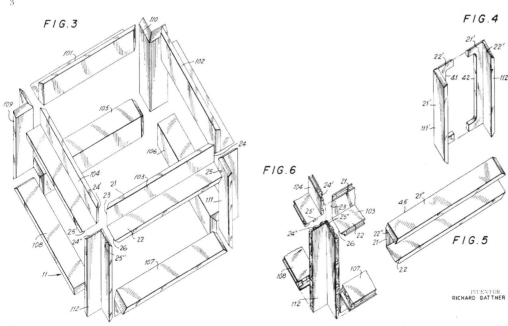

FIG.3

FIG.4

FIG.6

FIG.5

INVENTOR.
RICHARD DATTNER

4

5 Entrance deck and masonry chimney attach
  to frames
6 Frames can be erected without mechanical lifts
7 Living room with stair to sleeping loft
8 View from sleeping loft

5

6

7

8

PlayCubes

Design/Completion 1976/1977
U.S., Canada, U.K., Japan, Israel, Greece
PlayStreet/2001 Incorporated
Fiberglass-reinforced polyester modular units, tunnels, and slides

These patented, 14-sided cuboctahedrons have six square sides with round openings, and eight triangular sides. Linking these modules creates a safe and attractive play environment where children have opportunities for great freedom of movement and free rein to their imaginations. The colorful PlayCubes are light in weight, rigid, and capable of supporting connecting tunnels and slides. PlayCubes were manufactured and installed throughout the world.

1

2

238

1 Kids climb through, or over, the PlayCubes
2 Installation in a nursery school
3 Children are free to exercise their imaginations
4 Habitot unit preceded the PlayCubes design

3

4

Firm Profile

Richard Dattner & Partners Architects

Biographies of Principals

Richard Dattner, FAIA

Richard Dattner was born in Poland, from which his family emigrated, first to Italy and then to Cuba, where Mr. Dattner spent his early childhood. After World War II, his family came to the United States, where Mr. Dattner grew up in Buffalo, New York. He attended the Massachusetts Institute of Technology, initially studying engineering, then architecture. He attended the Architectural Association in London in 1957–58 and subsequently returned to MIT, where he received his Bachelor of Architecture degree in 1960.

Mr. Dattner established his practice in 1964, after serving in the U.S. Army Corps of Engineers and working in several New York City architectural firms. As the firm's founder and lead designer, he has been responsible for designing a wide variety of project types, including urban design, industrial, transportation, commercial, recreation, education, and residential buildings. His distinctive approach to design responds to the unique requirements of each project, and emphasizes the public context of buildings. His work balances architectural expression with the needs of users, the available technical means, and the realities of budget and time.

Early projects included private homes, the Adventure Playground in Central Park, and a manufacturing plant for Estée Lauder, Inc. on Long Island. Estée Lauder, Inc. has remained a client for over 35 years; Mr. Dattner has designed subsequent manufacturing plants, distribution centers, and corporate offices for the company in the Unites States, Canada, and Europe. Mr. Dattner designed a series of innovative public schools, including Intermediate School 195, built as part of a large housing development in Harlem, Public School 234 in the Tribeca neighborhood of Manhattan, and Intermediate School 218 in Washington Heights, hailed as "the school of the future". The firm won first prize in the recent "School of the Future" competition.

Mr. Dattner has designed a variety of recreational projects, including the Columbia University Stadium, Riverbank State Park, Asphalt Green AquaCenter, the Goodwill Games Swimming and Diving Complex, and the Pottruck Health and Fitness Center at the University of Pennsylvania. Other notable projects include the Prototype Intermediate Schools for New York City, the Hertz Rental Car facility in Orlando, Fl., the Rehabilitation of the West 72nd St. Subway Station, and the new Children's Center for the NYC Administration for Children's Services—the adaptive re-use and restoration of a landmark McKim Mead & White building.

In addition to his architectural work, Mr. Dattner has a distinguished record in product and industrial design. Early in his career, he designed a prefabricated, modular housing system, which was implemented in two demonstration houses. He designed the *Playcubes*™ modular fiberglass play system, now used in playgrounds around the world. Mr. Dattner developed a series of transit shelter designs and designed the *Streetscape*™ modular shelter and kiosk system— widely used as security booths, parking lot booths and news stands. He also designed *Shelterscape*™, a flexible, modular canopy system, which has been used at airports, recreational facilities and parking lots. Mr. Dattner holds patents for these designs and licenses their manufacture.

Mr. Dattner received the 1992 Medal of Honor from the American Institute of Architects (AIA), New York Chapter, and the 1994 Thomas Jefferson Award for Public Architecture from the American Institute of Architects. In 1999, he was honored by the Cultural Landscapes Foundation as a Pioneer of Modern Urban Landscape Design, in recognition of his Adventure Playgrounds in Central Park and other urban locations. His firm's work has received over 100 design awards and citations, including the AIA Honor Award, Bard Award of the City Club of New York, AIA New York State Design Awards, New York City Art Commission Awards, and the Urban Land Institute Award.

Mr. Dattner was elected a Fellow of the American Institute of Architects in 1981. He served as Vice-President of the AIA New York Chapter in 1986–88 and 1996–98, and has been a member of the Fellows, Transportation and Public Sectors Contracts Committees.

He has been a member of the Board on Infrastructure and the Constructed Environment of the National Research Council, served on the White House Conference on Children in 1970, and was a member of the Advisory Board of the American Revolution Bicentennial Commission in 1976. He served on Community Board 12 in Manhattan, and is a former Trustee of the City Club of New York. He is a Fellow of the Institute for Urban Design.

Mr. Dattner has been Distinguished Visiting Professor of Architecture at the University of Wisconsin (1982), Adjunct Professor of Architecture at the City College of New York (1970–80) and Adjunct Professor of Architecture at the Cooper Union (1962–69). He has been a guest critic and lecturer at Columbia University, Princeton University, Cornell University, City University of New York, University of Cali in Colombia, National Institute for Architectural Education, and the Massachusetts Institute of Technology.

Richard Dattner is the author of *Design for Play* (Van Nostrand/Reinhold, 1969), a study of the ways in which children play and interact in playgrounds, with a survey of playground design. He is the author of *Civil Architecture: The New Public Infrastructure* (McGraw-Hill, 1995), a study of contemporary trends in the design of public buildings and the balance between the private and public realms in society.

Mr. Dattner is registered in New York, New Jersey, Connecticut, Pennsylvania and Florida, and holds a certificate from the National Council of Architectural Registration Boards.

Joseph Coppola, AIA

Joseph Coppola was born in Buseto Palizzolo, Sicily. His family emigrated to the United States when he was seven years old, and he was raised in Brooklyn and Queens, New York. He attended the City College of New York and received a Bachelor of Architecture in 1972. He has studied real estate finance and network administration at New York University.

Mr. Coppola joined Richard Dattner & Associates in 1977, after working for several New York City firms. He was named an Associate in 1980, a Senior Associate in 1987, and became a Principal of the firm in 1999. His thoughtful, detailed approach to design and project development has resulted in buildings of outstanding architectural quality.

Mr. Coppola has managed projects including a Con Edison Service Building, the new Children's Center for the NYC Administration for Children's Services, the Goodwill Games Swimming and Diving Complex, Asphalt Green AquaCenter, Louis Armstrong Cultural Center, Riverbank State Park, Estée Lauder Corporate Offices, Whitney Museum Interiors, Jewish Museum Coins and Medals Exhibit, Manhattan 1 and 2 Theaters, Striebel Residence, and Soros offices. In addition to his project responsibilities, Mr. Coppola manages the firm's technology systems and guides the firm's use of computers and electronic networks.

Mr. Coppola is a member of the American Institute of Architects and, at the AIA New York Chapter, has served on the Historic Buildings and Computer Committees. He is registered in New York, and holds a certificate from the National Council of Architectural Registration Boards.

William Stein, AIA

William Stein was born in Washington, DC and raised in Queens, New York and Cleveland, Ohio. He attended Hamilton College and received the Bachelor of Arts in Humanities from the New School for Social Research. He attended the City College of New York, and received a Bachelor of Architecture in 1977.

Mr. Stein joined Richard Dattner & Associates in 1979, after working for several New York City firms and as a Facilities Administrator for the City University of New York. He was named an Associate in 1980, a Senior Associate in 1987, and became a Principal of the firm in 1999. His collaborative approach builds consensus among participants and users to achieve design excellence within the constraints of the public design and construction process.

Mr. Stein has managed a wide variety of projects, including the Estée Lauder Automated Warehouse Facility, Con Edison Customer Service Centers, Columbia University Stadium, Public School 234, Intermediate School 218, the Parkchester and Cypress Hills Branch Libraries, the 1992 Democratic National Convention, the Eastchester Gardens Community Center, and the 33rd Precinct Station House for the New York Police Department. He manages the firm's transit projects, including the West 72nd St, Queensboro Plaza, Pelham Parkway, and West 42nd St/8th Ave. Subway Station Rehabilitations. He has directed a variety of projects for the Port Authority of New York and New Jersey at JFK and Newark International Airports, and at the World Trade Center. Residential projects include six senior citizens residences for the New York Foundation for Senior Citizens, housing for the mentally ill, homeless, and special needs populations. In addition to his project responsibilities, he oversees the firm's business development and marketing programs.

Mr. Stein is a member of the American Institute of Architects. He served as a Director of the AIA New York Chapter (1990–92), co-authoring the Chapter's *Long Range Plan* and By-Laws revisions, and has served as chair of the Finance, Continuing Education, and Public Sector Contracts Committees. As President of the New York Foundation for Architecture in 1998, he led the Foundation's transition to a more activist, prominent role in promoting public awareness of architecture and the built environment. He is a member of the AIA New York Chapter's Zoning Task Force.

Mr. Stein is registered in New York and New Jersey, and holds a certificate from the National Council of Architectural Registration Boards.

Bernard Zipprich, AIA

Bernard Zipprich was born and raised in Staten Island, New York. He attended the Catholic University of America in Washington, DC, receiving a Bachelor of Science in Architecture in 1974 and a Master in Architecture in 1976. In 1973 he attended the University's Foreign Studies program in Italy.

Mr. Zipprich joined Richard Dattner & Associates as an Associate in 1987. He was named a Senior Associate in 1993, and became a Principal of the firm in 1999. From 1982 to 1987, he held the positions of Administrative Architect and Project Manager with Columbia University. He previously worked for architectural firms and organizations in Washington, DC and New York City. His ability to organize, manage and implement complex projects has been key to the realization of a wide range of public and private buildings.

Mr. Zipprich has managed education and university projects, including the Prototype Intermediate Schools (IS 2, IS 5, IS 90 and IS 171), the Maxwell High School Modernization and Addition, the Pfizer School Renovation, Brooklyn College Dining Facilities and Learning Center projects, Columbia University Athletic Facilities, and Columbia University School of Social Work Alteration. Other projects he has directed include the Hertz Car Rental and Service Facility in Orlando, Fl., projects for the New York Athletic Club, the Reconstruction of Firehouses for the NYC Fire Department, the new Engine Company 75/Ladder Company 33, and the Renovation of the Thomas Jefferson Pool and Bathhouse. He has managed multiple capital improvement contracts for New York City schools, representing renovations at over 50 public schools. In addition to his project responsibilities, Mr. Zipprich oversees human resources management activities for the firm.

He is a member of the American Institute of Architects and, at the AIA New York Chapter, has served as Chair of the Public Sector Contracts Committee. He has been a member of the Joint Advisory Committee for the Continental Village Park District in Putnam County, New York. Mr. Zipprich is registered in New York and New Jersey.

Beth Greenberg, AIA

Beth Greenberg was born and raised in Omaha, Nebraska. She attended the University of Wisconsin at Madison, receiving a Bachelor of Science in French and Dance Education. She received a Master of Architecture from the University of Colorado, Denver in 1983.

Ms. Greenberg joined Richard Dattner & Associates in 1989, was named an Associate in 1993, and became a Principal in 1999. Her previous work included management of a new, mixed-use, high-rise condominium waterfront community in New Jersey, an AIA-honored custom single-family home, alterations to a Denver Sports Arena, and office/research buildings. Ms. Greenberg's ability to integrate the needs of users with the technical requirements of complex public projects has resulted in buildings that benefit their clients and communities.

She has managed projects including the Leake & Watts Family Services Cottages and School, Children's Discovery Center at The New York Botanical Garden, the 1992 Democratic National Convention improvements at Madison Square Garden, and construction administration for Riverbank State Park. She led the team for the design competition for the NYC Police Training Facility. She managed the new Public School 15 in Yonkers, NY and the Goodwill Games Swimming and Diving Complex. Other notable projects include Modular School Additions, the Flanzer Eye Clinic and Children's Pulmonary Center at New York Presbyterian Medical Center, Project Return Housing for Women and Children, a new stadium at the State University of New York at Stony Brook, and the Pottruck Health and Fitness Center at the University of Pennsylvania. In addition to her project responsibilities, Ms. Greenberg directs the firm's professional development programs.

Ms. Greenberg is a member of the American Institute of Architects and, at the AIA New York Chapter, has served as Chair of the Housing Committee and on the *Oculus* Committee, overseeing the Chapter's publication. She helped to organize Crosstown/116, an urban-planning initiative of the AIA New York Chapter, which brought together architects, students, and community members to develop design ideas for a major Harlem thoroughfare.

Ms. Greenberg was a Guest Lecturer at the New York State Office of General Services Minority Construction Management State Internship Program, served as Editor of the *Women in Architecture Newsletter* in Denver, Colorado, and as a Board Member of the Denver Urban Design Forum. She is registered in New York, and holds a certificate from the National Council of Architectural Registration Boards.

Architectural Awards and Exhibitions

2000 **Public Art Exhibition**
New York City Department of Design
and Construction
Administration for Children's Services
Children's Center
Engine Company 75

1999 **Facility of Merit Award**
Athletic Business Magazine
The Goodwill Games Swimming and
Diving Complex

1999 **New York City Art Commission Award
for Excellence in Design**
New York City Art Commission
Administration for Children's Services
New Children's Center

1999 **NYACE Structural/Building Platinum
Award**
New York Association of Consulting
Engineers, Inc.
Goodwill Games Swimming and Diving
Complex

1998 **Open Space Award**
Landmark West!
Adventure Playground

1997 **First Prize: "School Commons Looking
to the Future" Design Competition**
New York City School Construction
Authority
Prototypical Designs for shared space
in public schools

1997 **Merit Award with Special Recognition**
The Concrete Industry Board, Inc.
Goodwill Games Swimming and Diving
Complex

1997 **First Prize: "Classroom of the Future"
Design Competition**
New York City School Construction
Authority
Prototypical Designs for the Classroom
of the Future

1997 **21st Century Streetscape Exhibition**
Municipal Art Society
Intermodal Transit Shelter

1997 **New York City Art Commission Award
for Excellence in Design**
New York City Art Commission
Rehabilitation of Four Fire Department
Station Houses

1996 **Honorable Mention Award for
Excellence in Design**
National Council on Seniors' Housing
Concourse Gardens

1996 **Civics Lessons Exhibition**
American Institute of Architects
New York Chapter
Queensboro Plaza Station
Riverbank State Park
Sludge Dewatering Facilities
Intermediate School 218
Intermediate School 2

1996 **Honorable Mention, Environments**
I.D. Annual Design Review
Hertz Orlando Airport Facility

1996 **New York City Art Commission Award
for Excellence in Design**
New York City Art Commission
The Children's Adventure Garden
Discovery Center
The New York Botanical Garden

1995 **New York City Public Works 100 Years
Exhibit**
The Municipal Engineers of the City
of New York
The New York City Department of
General Services
Louis Armstrong Cultural Center
Cypress Hills Library

1995 **Urban Land Institute Award**
Urban Land Institute
Riverbank State Park

1995 **Award of Merit**
The Concrete Institute Board, Inc.
New York City DEP Sludge Storage
Buildings

1995 **New Architecture in Brooklyn
Exhibition**
The Rotunda Gallery
Intermediate School 2
Coney Island Lifeguard/Comfort
Stations

1995 **Pillars of the Industry Award**
National Association of Home Builders
Clinton Gardens Housing

1994 **Excellence in Design Award**
American Institute of Architects
New York State
Asphalt Green AquaCenter

1994 **Thomas Jefferson Award
for Public Architecture**
American Institute of Architects

1994 **Philip N. Winslow Design Award for
Landscape Architecture**
The Parks Council
Riverbank State Park

1994 **Design of Merit Award**
Concrete Industry Board of New York
Sludge Dewatering Facilities

1994 **Facility of Merit Award**
Athletic Business Magazine
Riverbank State Park

1994 **New York City Art Commission Award
for Excellence in Design**
New York City Art Commission
Sludge Dewatering Facilities

1994 **New York Waterfront Exhibition**
The Cooper Union
Riverbank State Park
West 59th St. Marine Transfer Station
Sherman Creek State Park
Hudson Riverfront Study

1994 **Best of Senior's Housing Award**
National Council on Senior's Housing
Ridge Street Gardens

1993 **New York State AIA Award**
American Institute of Architects
New York State
Riverbank State Park

1993 **Steel Institute Award**
The Steel Institute of New York
Riverbank State Park

1993 **Masonry Institute Award**
Masonry Institute of New York
Intermediate School 218

1993 **Leader of Industry Award**
Concrete Industry Board
Various Projects

1993 **New York City Police Academy
Exhibition**
The Municipal Art Society

1993 **New York City Police Academy
Exhibition**
Pratt Institute

1992 **Second Prize**
New York City
Department of General Services
Police Academy Competition

1992 **Medal of Honor**
American Institute of Architects
New York Chapter

1992 **Fifth Annual Honor Award**
The Construction Specifications
Institute
Prototype Intermediate School 2,
Brooklyn

1991 **First Prize Bronze Plaque**
Queens Chamber of Commerce
Public School 11 Mini School

1991 **Bronze Citation, Educational Interiors**
American School & University
Magazine
Brooklyn College Dining Facility

1990 **Garbage Out Front Exhibition**
The Municipal Art Society
West 59th Street Marine Transfer
Station

1990 **First Prize, Engineering Excellence**
Association of Consulting Engineers
New York
Riverbank State Park Bridges

1989 **Award of Merit**
Concrete Industry Board of New York
Public School 234

1989 **Architectural Portfolio 1989**
American School & University
Magazine
Public School 234

1989 **New York State/AIA Honorable Mention
Award**
American Institute of Architects
New York State
Public School 234

1989 **Outstanding Service Award**
New York Building Congress
Prototype Intermediate Schools

1989 **Bard Award for Excellence in
Architecture**
The City Club of New York
Public School 234

1989 **New York City Art Commission Award
for Excellence in Design**
New York City Art Commission
Prototype Intermediate Schools

1989 **Parks Council Public Service Award**
The Parks Council
Public School 234

1989 **Prototype Schools Exhibition**
American Institute of Architects New
York Chapter
Prototype Intermediate Schools

1988 **New York City Art Commission Award
for Excellence in Design**
New York City Art Commission
Cunningham Park Master Plan

1988 **New York City Percent for Art Exhibition**
New York City Department of Cultural Affairs
Public School 234
West 59th St.
Marine Transfer Station

1987 **New York State/AIA Award**
American Institute of Architects/New York State
Automated Warehouse

1987 **Evolution of the Playground Exhibition**
New York City Parks and Recreation
Central Park Projects

1987 **Computer Images of Architecture**
American Institute of Architects
New York Chapter
Various Projects

1987 **New York Exhibition**
The Queens Museum
Riverbank State Park

1985 **New York City Art Commission Award for Excellence in Design**
New York City Art Commission
Public School 234

1984 **Albert S. Bard Award**
The City Club of New York
Central Park Projects

1984 **Architectural Portfolio 1984**
American School & University Magazine
Lawrence A. Wien Stadium
Columbia University

1984 **Contract Award**
Cunningham Park Competition
New York City Parks Department

1984 **Award, Institutional Category**
Concrete Industry Board
Lawrence A. Wien Stadium
Columbia University

1983 **New York City Art Commission Award for Excellence in Design**
New York City Art Commission
Riverbank State Park Bridges

1982 **Overseas Architecture Exhibition**
American Institute of Architects
Estée Lauder Laboratories, Switzerland

1982 **Culture Stations Exhibition**
Municipal Art Society
Lincoln Center 66th St. Station

1980 **Solar Pioneer Award**
United States Department of Energy
National Children's Island

1979 **Architecture Alumni Exhibition**
The Massachusetts Institute of Technology
Various Projects

1979 **Transformations in Modern Architecture Exhibition**
The Museum of Modern Art
Estée Lauder Laboratories

1978 **Honor Award in Engineering**
New York Association of Consulting Engineers
National Children's Island

1978 **Election to College of Fellows**
American Institute of Architects

1978 **Celebration of Water Exhibit**
Cooper-Hewitt Museum
Various Projects

1977 **Design Review**
Whitney Library of Art
Streetscape Modular Shelters

1977 **Design Award**
Westchester Municipal Planning Federation
Cerrato Park

1977 **Theater Design '77 Exhibit**
United States Institute for Theater Technology
National Children's Island Amphitheater

1977 **Award, Mixed-Use Category**
Concrete Industry Board
Riverside Park Community/Intermediate School 195

1977 **Living Space Exhibition**
Studio Museum of Harlem
Riverside Park Community

1976 **Contract Award Finalist**
Playground For All Children Competition
City of New York

1976 **Urban Amenities Award**
Concrete Institute Board of New York
Cerrato Park

1976 **Architecture Permanent Collection**
Studio Museum of Harlem
Riverside Park Community

1976 **Architectural Record Interiors**
Architectural Record Magazine
New York Apartment

1975 **Cortlandt Town Hall Competition, First Prize**
Town of Cortlandt, New York

1975 **Design Award**
Progressive Architecture Magazine
Sherman Creek State Park

1973 **20th Annual Design Review**
Industrial Design Magazine
Ancient Play Garden

1972 **19th Annual Design Review**
Industrial Design Magazine
Modular House

1971 **Fiberglas is Fun Exhibit**
Owens-Corning Fiberglas
PlayCubes Modular Playground

1971 **18th Annual Design Review**
Industrial Design Magazine
Rehabilitation Playground,
New York University Medical Center

1971 **Art for Public Places Exhibit 1971**
University of Washington, Seattle
Playgrounds

1971 **AIA Honor Award**
American Institute of Architects
Estée Lauder Laboratories

1970 **Industrial Design Review**
Chicago Museum of Science and Industry
PlayCubes Modular Playground

1970 **17th Annual Design Review**
Industrial Design Magazine
East 72nd St. Playground

1970 **Honor Award**
The American Society of Landscape Architects
Private Residence

1970 **Traveling Exhibit: Architecture USA**
United States Information Agency
Estée Lauder Laboratories

1969 **16th Annual Design Review**
Industrial Design Magazine
PlayCubes Modular Playground

1968 **Design Review Exhibition**
The Smithsonian Institute
Lower Playground

1968 **15th Annual Design Review**
Industrial Design Magazine
Lower Playground

1968 **Second Prize, Engineering Excellence Competition**
Association of Consulting Engineers New York
Estée Lauder Laboratories

1968 **Certificate of Commendation**
Park Association of New York City
Adventure Playground

1968 **Environment Award**
American Institute of Architects New York Chapter
Adventure Playground

1967 **Design Review Exhibition**
The Brooklyn Museum
Adventure Playground

1967 **Grand Prize, Industrial Category**
Long Island Association
Estée Lauder Laboratories

1967 **14th Annual Design Review**
Industrial Design Magazine
Adventure Playground
81st Street Playground

1967 **Hudson Riverfront Exhibit**
American Institute of Architects
New York Chapter
Hudson Riverfront Study

Clients

Corporate
Aramis
Benerofe Properties
Camp Dresser & McKee
Cinema 5 Ltd.
Clinique Laboratories
Columbia Cascade Timber Company
Consolidated Edison
Estée Lauder Inc.
Estée Lauder International
First Investors Corporation
Grayco Development and Construction
    Corp.
Greeley & Hansen
Hardesty & Hanover Consulting Engineers
Hastings Associates
Hazen & Sawyer
Hertz Corporation
Imobiliare, USA
New York City 2012 Olympic Committee
Norden Systems
NYNEX
Origins, Inc.
Parsons Brinckerhoff Quade & Douglas
Pfizer Corporation
Prescriptives, Inc.
Red Hook Planning
Republic National Bank
Rockrose Development Corp.
Soros Fund Management
Stone & Webster
Streetscape Inc.
Time Warner Cable Inc.
Triglia Development
Webb and Brooker
Whitman Laboratories, UK

Institutions
The Berkeley Carroll School
Brooklyn College
Brooklyn Public Library
Cabrini Medical Center
The Center School
City College of New York
City University Law School
City University of New York
Columbia University
Columbia University School of Social
    Work
Congregation Rodeph Sholom
Democratic National Convention
    Committee
Goodwill Games 1998
Hunter College & Hunter College Campus
    School

Intrepid Museum
Jewish Community Center of Staten Island
The Jewish Museum
Mount Sinai Hospital
New York Athletic Club
The New York Botanical Garden
New York Hall of Science
New York Presbyterian Hospital
The New York Public Library
New York University
New York University Medical Center
Riverdale Neighborhood House
Rutgers University
Takapausha Museum
The Stony Brook School
Queens College
Whitney Museum of American Art
State University of New York at Stony
    Brook
University of Pennsylvania

Local Government
City of Jerusalem
City of Tel Aviv
Community Development Agency,
    Newark, NJ
Community Development Agency,
    Yonkers, NY
District of Columbia
Metropolitan Development Agency,
    Tampa, FL
Model Cities, Highland Park, MI
Model Cities, Rochester, NY
Nassau County Parks & Recreation
Town of Cortlandt, NY
Town of Secaucus, NJ
Union Free School District 13
Yonkers Public Schools

New York City
Manhattan Borough President
NYC Board of Education
NYC Dept. of City Planning
NYC Dept. of Design and Construction
NYC Dept. of Environmental Protection
NYC Dept. of Housing, Preservation &
    Development
NYC Dept. of Sanitation
NYC Economic Development Corporation
NYC Educational Construction Fund
NYC Fire Department
NYC Housing Authority
NYC Parks & Recreation
NYC Police Department
NYC School Construction Authority
Queens Borough President

Not-For-Profit Organizations
14th Street Merchants Association
Asphalt Green Inc.
Beginning With Children Inc.
Bellevue Association
Camp Rising Sun
Estée and Joseph Lauder Foundation
Federation Employment Guidance
    Services
J.M. Kaplan Fund
Jewish Board of Family and Children's
    Services
Jewish Board of Guardians
Leake and Watts Family Services
Metropolitan Coordinating Council on
    Jewish Poverty
National Children's Island Inc.
New York Foundation for Senior Citizens
Phipps Houses
Playground Association/85th Street
Project Find
Project Return Foundation Inc.
Services for the Underserved
Sheltering Arms Children's Services
Washington Heights & Inwood
    Development Corp.
Washington Heights Chamber of
    Commerce
Westchester Association for Retarded
    Citizens
Weston United Community Renewal, Inc.

State and Federal Government
Empire State Development Corporation
MTA/New York City Transit
NYS Division of Housing and Community
    Renewal
NYS Dormitory Authority
NYS Office of General Services
NYS Office of Mental Health
NYS Office of Parks, Recreation & Historic
    Preservation
NYS Urban Development Corporation
Port Authority of New York & New Jersey
State University Construction Fund
United States Army Corps of Engineers
United States Postal Service

Chronological List of Selected Buildings and Projects

*Indicates work featured in this book

*Estée Lauder Laboratories (1)
Melville, New York
Estée Lauder Companies
1964–72

*Central Park Playgrounds
New York, New York
Lauder Foundation, New York City
Parks & Recreation
1966

*Modular House
Amagansett, New York
Private Residence
1969

*Primary School PS 380, Brooklyn
Brooklyn, New York
New York City Board of Education
1969–80

Riverside Park Community
New York, New York
Negro Labor Committee
1970

*Sherman Creek State Park
New York, New York
New York State Office of Parks,
Recreation, & Historic Preservation
1972

Estée Lauder Laboratories
Toronto, Canada
Estée Lauder Companies
1972

Riverfront Park
Tampa, Florida
Tampa Model Cities Administration
1973

National Children's Island
Washington, DC
National Children's Island
1975

*Automated Storage Retrieval Facility (2)
Melville, New York
Estée Lauder Companies
1976–80

Whitman Laboratories
Petersfield, U.K.
Estée Lauder Companies
1977

*Riverbank State Park (3)
New York, New York
New York State Office of Parks,
Recreation & Historic Preservation
1978–93

*Streetscape Modular Shelters
Various Locations
2001 Incorporated
1978

*Con Edison Customer Service Facility
Bronx, New York
Con Edison, Benerofe Properties
1978–80

*Columbia University Stadium
New York, New York
Columbia University
1979–84

Parfums Stern Manufacturing Facility
Happaugue, New York
Parfums Stern, Inc.
1981

66th St. Lincoln Center Station
New York, New York
MTA New York City Transit
1982

*Parkchester Branch Library (4)
Bronx, New York
The New York Public Library
1982

*Estée Lauder Research Laboratories
Melville, New York
Estée Lauder Companies
1983–98

1

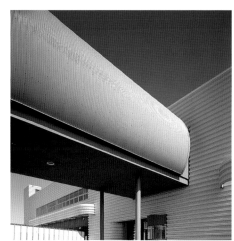
2

3

Marine Transfer Station, Greenpoint
Brooklyn, New York
New York City Department of Sanitation, Ebasco
1984

Thomas Jefferson Pool Center
New York, New York
New York City Parks & Recreation
1984

*Primary School PS 234, Manhattan (5)
New York, New York
New York City Board of Education
1984

Marine Transfer Station, W. 59th St. (6)
New York, New York
New York City Department of Sanitation, Greeley & Hansen
1984

*Marine Transfer Station, W. 135th St.
New York, New York
New York City Department of Sanitation, Greeley & Hansen
1984–87

*Intrepid Park & Museum
New York, New York
Intrepid Museum Memorial
1985

*Intermediate School IS 218, Manhattan
New York, New York
New York City Board of Education, New York City School Construction Authority
1985

*Townsend Harris Hall, City College
New York, New York
City University of New York,
Dormitory Authority of the State of New York
1985

*Brooklyn College Dining Facility
Brooklyn, New York
City University of New York
1985

*Louis Armstrong Cultural Center
Queens, New York
Elmcor, New York City Department of Design & Construction
1987

*Intermediate School IS 2, Brooklyn
Brooklyn, New York
New York City Board of Education, New York City School Construction Authority
1988

*Intermediate School IS 5, Queens
Queens, New York
New York City Board of Education, New York City School Construction Authority
1988

*Intermediate School IS 90, Manhattan
New York, New York
New York City Board of Education, New York City School Construction Authority
1988

*Cypress Hills Branch Library
Brooklyn, New York
Brooklyn Public Library
1988

*26th Ward Sludge Treatment Facility
Brooklyn, New York
New York City Department of Environmental Protection, Hazen & Sawyer, Stone & Webster
1989–96

*Asphalt Green AquaCenter (7)
New York, New York
Asphalt Green, Inc.,
New York City Parks & Recreation
1989

Hunts Point Sludge Treatment Facility
Bronx, New York
New York City Department of Environmental Protection, Hazen & Sawyer, Stone & Webster
1989

4

5

6

Jamaica Bay Sludge Treatment Facility
Bronx, New York
New York City Department of
Environmental Protection, Hazen
& Sawyer, Stone & Webster
1989

*Estée Lauder Corporate Headquarters
New York, New York
Estée Lauder Companies
1989–95

*Oakwood Beach Sludge Treatment
Facility
Staten Island, New York
New York City Department of
Environmental Protection, Hazen &
Sawyer, Stone & Webster
1989–92

*Bowery Bay Sewage Treatment Facility (8)
Queens, New York
New York City Department of
Environmental Protection, Hazen
& Sawyer, Stone & Webster
1989–2000

*Wards Island Sludge Treatment Facility
New York, New York
New York City Department of
Environmental Protection, Hazen
& Sawyer, Stone & Webster
1989–95

*Tallman Island Sludge Treatment Facility
Queens, New York
New York City Department of
Environmental Protection, Hazen
& Sawyer, Stone & Webster
1989–92

*Rainbow Bridge U.S. Plaza
Niagara Falls, New York
U.S. Customs, Hardesty & Hanover
1990

*Clinton Gardens (9)
New York, New York
New York Foundation for Senior Citizens,
US Dept of Housing & Urban Development
1990

*Ridge Street Gardens
New York, New York
New York Foundation for Senior Citizens,
US Dept of Housing & Urban Development
1990

Distribution Warehouse
Upper McCungie, Pennsylvania
Lane-Webber Inc.
1990

Journal Square Terminal Improvements
Jersey City, New Jersey
Port Authority of New York and New Jersey
1992

*Democratic National Convention
New York, New York
New York City Economic Development
Corporation, Democratic National
Convention Committee
1992

Starhill Residence Additions
Bronx, New York
Project Return Foundation, Inc.
1992–96

*Maxwell High School
Brooklyn, New York
New York City Board of Education
New York City School Construction
Authority
1992

*Roundtop at Montrose
Cortlandt, New York
Triglia Development
1992–2000

*New York City Police Academy
Bronx, New York
New York City Department of Design
& Construction,
New York City Police Department
1992

*Leake & Watts School and Residences
Yonkers, New York
Leake & Watts Family Services
1993–98

7

8

9

Abraham Residence III
New York, New York
New York State Office of Mental Health
Metropolitan Council on Jewish Poverty
1993

*Con Edison Gas System Control Room
Bronx, New York
Consolidated Edison
1993

Eastchester Gardens Community Center
Bronx, New York
New York City Housing Authority
1994–98

Hill House Residence
Bronx, New York
Project Return Foundation, Inc.
1994–99

Modernization of the Brownsville Houses
Brooklyn, New York
New York City Housing Authority
1994–98

***Whitney Museum of American Art
Exhibition**
New York, New York
Whitney Museum of American Art
1994

*Hertz Orlando Airport Facility (10)
Orlando, Florida
Hertz Corporation
1994–96

*Con Edison Customer Service Facility (11)
Brooklyn, New York
Consolidated Edison
1994–97

***Goodwill Games Swimming and Diving
Complex** (12)
East Meadow, New York
Dormitory Authority
of the State of New York
Nassau County Parks & Recreation
1994–98

*Columbia University School of Social Work
New York, New York
Columbia University
1994

*Flanzer Eye Clinic
New York, New York
New York Presbyterian Medical Center
1996

Rodeph Sholom School
New York, New York
Congregation Rodeph Sholom
1996–98

*Coney Island Lifeguard Stations
Brooklyn, New York
U.S. Army Corps of Engineers
New York City Parks & Recreation
1994

*Berkeley Carroll School Athletic Center
Brooklyn, New York
The Berkeley Carroll School
1995–2000

***JFK International Airport IAB Renewal
Project**
Queens, New York
Port Authority of New York & New Jersey
1994

*Queensboro Plaza Station
Queens, New York
MTA New York City Transit
1994–2000

*Shelterscape Modular System
Various Locations
2001 Incorporated, Northern Plastics
1995

*Catskill-Delaware Filtration Facility
Westchester, New York
Hazen & Sawyer, Camp Dresser & McKee
New York City Department of
Environmental Protection
1995–2000

10

11

12

*The New York Botanical Garden Discovery Center
Bronx, New York
New York Botanical Garden,
Miceli, Kulik, Williams
1995

*33rd Police Precinct House (13)
New York, New York
NYC Department of Design &
Construction,
New York City Police Department
1995–2000

*New York Athletic Club Pool (14)
New York, New York
New York Athletic Club
1995–98

Concourse Gardens
Bronx, New York
New York Foundation for Senior Citizens
1995

*Intermodal Transfer Shelters
Various Locations
MTA New York City Transit
Parsons Brinckerhoff Quade & Douglas
1996

*72nd Street Station, Broadway (15)
New York, New York
MTA New York City Transit
1996–2003

*River View Gardens
Queens, New York
New York Foundation for Senior Citizens
1996–2001

*Estée Lauder Distribution Center
Lachen, Switzerland
Estée Lauder Companies
1996–98 (Phase 2)
1975–97 (Phase 1)

*Pediatric Lung Center
New York, New York
New York Presbyterian Medical Center
1996

*Stony Brook Stadium
Stony Brook, New York
State University of New York
1997–2001

*Primary School 15, Yonkers
Yonkers, New York
Yonkers Board of Education
1997

*ACS Children's Center (16)
New York, New York
Agency for Children's Services,
New York City Dept of General Services
1997–2000

*Brooklyn District Garages 1 & 4
Brooklyn, New York
New York City Dept of Sanitation
1997–2001

*Engine Company 75 Firehouse
Bronx, New York
New York City Dept of Design
& Construction
New York City Fire Department
1997–2000

*Paerdegat Basin CSO Facility
Brooklyn, New York
New York City Dept of Environmental
Protection
Hazen & Sawyer
1997–2002

*Amtrak/Long Island Railroad Ventilation Structures
Manhattan and Queens, New York
Amtrak/Long Island Railroad,
Parsons Brinckerhoff Quade & Douglas
1997–2001

*Alma Rangel Gardens
New York, New York
New York Foundation for Senior Citizens
1997–2001

13

14

15

*Jewish Community Center of Staten
Island
Staten Island, New York
JCC of Staten Island
1998

*Con Edison Service Building (17)
New York, New York
Consolidated Edison
1998

Coney Island Community Center
Brooklyn, New York
New York City Housing Authority
1998–2001

*42nd Street/8th Avenue Station
New York, New York
MTA New York City Transit
1998–2002

*Pelham Parkway Station
Bronx, New York
MTA New York City Transit
1998–2002

*University of Pennsylvania Health
& Fitness Center
Philadelphia, Pennsylvania
University of Pennsylvania
1999

*Modular Schools
Queens, New York
New York City Board of Education
New York City School Construction
Authority
1998

*Newark International Airport Vertical
Transportation (18)
Newark, New Jersey
The Port Authority of New York
& New Jersey
1999

Primary School PS 178, Manhattan
New York, New York
New York City Board of Education,
New York City School Construction
Authority
Calcedo Construction
2000

Primary School PS 228, Queens
New York, New York
New York City Board of Education,
New York City School Construction
Authority,
Citnalta Construction
2000

Arverne Edgemere Houses Improvements
Queens, New York
New York City Housing Authority
2000

16

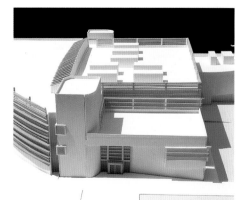
17

18

Publications

The work of Richard Dattner & Partners Architects appears in the following publications.

Selected Books

Carles, Broto. *Commercial Spaces.* Barcelona: LINKS International, 1997

Civics Lessons: Recent New York Public Architecture. New York: AIA New York Chapter, 1997

Dattner, Richard. *Civil Architecture—The New Public Infrastructure.* New York: McGraw-Hill, 1995

Dattner, Richard. *Design for Play.* New York: Van Nostrand/Reinhold, 1969, Cambridge: MIT Press, 1974

Design Review, 23rd Annual. New York: The Whitney Library of Design, 1977

Dickinson, Duo. *The Small House.* New York: McGraw-Hill, 1986

Drexler, Arthur. *Transformations in Modern Architecture.* New York: The Museum of Modern Art, 1979

Garvin, Alexander; Berens, Gayle; et al. *Urban Parks and Open Space.* Washington, DC: The Urban Land Institute, 1997

Graves, Ben. *School Ways—The Planning and Design of America's Schools.* New York: McGraw-Hill, 1993

Grube, Oswald. *Industrial Buildings and Factories.* New York: Praeger Publishers, 1971

New Schools for New York. The Architectural League—Public Education Association. New York: Princeton Architectural Press, 1992

Pearlman, Hugh. *Contemporary World Architecture.* London: Phaidon Press, 1998

Preserving Modern Landscape Architecture. Cambridge: Spacemaker Press, 1999

Rifkind, Carole. *A Field Guide to Contemporary American Architecture.* New York: Penguin Publishers, 1998

Sirefman, Susanna. *New York.* London: Ellipsis Press, 1997

Spreiregen, Paul. *Design Competitions.* New York: McGraw-Hill, 1979

Stern, Robert et al. *New York 1960.* New York: The Monacelli Press, 1995

Water Spaces of the World. Australia: The Images Publishing Group, 1997

White, Norval, Willensky, Elliot et al. *AIA Guide to New York City.* New York: Harcourt Brace Jovanovich, 1988

Selected Journal Articles

Asphalt Green AquaCenter

"Live from New York." *Swim Magazine* (June, 1994)

"Manhattan Oasis." *The Architectural Review* (August, 1994)

Boylan Hall Dining Facility, Brooklyn College

"Brooklyn College Dining Facilities." *American School & University* (July, 1991)

Democratic National Convention 1992

"Stars, Stripes, and Spots." *Design Quarterly* (Fall, 1992)

"Up on the Convention Podiums, Star Spangled Symbolism." *The New York Times* (July 2, 1992)

Estée Lauder Corporate Headquarters

"Architects Collaborate to Create Worldwide Headquarters for Cosmetics Titan Estée Lauder." *Interior Design* (September, 1994)

Estée Lauder Laboratories

"Streamlined Factory: White Streak along the Open Road." *Architectural Forum* (March, 1967)

Goodwill Games Aquatic Facility

"Building a Gold Medal Pool." *Architectural Record* (March, 1999)

"1999 Architectural Showcase." *Athletic Business Magazine* (June, 1999)

"Soaring Trusses Frame Goodwill Games Aquatic Center." *Metals in Construction* (Spring, 1999)

Hertz Orlando Customer Service Facility

"We're Still Number 1." *Contract Design* (June, 1996)

Modular House

"A Modular House That's Different." *Architectural Forum* (October, 1972)

"Prefabricated House." *Architecture and Urbanism* (July, 1977)

"*Systeme Modulaire.*" *L'Architecture D'Aujourd'hui* (September, 1972)

Playground Projects

"Design for Play." *The Architect and Surveyor* (February, 1972)

"Four Playgrounds by Richard Dattner." *Architecture and Urbanism* (July, 1974)

"Playground Designs." *Industrial Design Magazine* (December, 1970, December, 1971)

"Playgrounds Shape Children Shape Playgrounds." *American City Magazine* (August, 1969)

"Play's the Thing." *Architectural Forum* (June, 1969)

"The Play's the Thing." *Newsweek* (December 27, 1971)

Prototype Intermediate Schools

"Prototype Schools Provide Urban Solution." *Building Design & Construction* (August, 1996)

Public School PS 234

"Learning Curve." *Architectural Record* (March, 1989)

"Primary Consideration." *Architectural Record Review* (1991)

Public School PS 380

"*Ecole Primaire a* Brooklyn, New York." *L'Architecture D'Aujourd'hui* (March, 1971)

Riverbank State Park

"Coney Island on the Hudson." *Time Magazine* (November 21, 1988)

"Harlem Gets a Sewage Plant ... and a Park." *Progressive Architecture* (October, 1993)

"Infrastructure Reconstructed." *Design Quarterly* (Winter, 1993)

"Project Reference File." *The Urban Land Institute* (March, 1996)

"Parks and Recreational Facilities." *Architectural Record* (November, 1993)

"Riverbank Park." *Contraspazio* (September, 1985)

Riverside Park Community

"Down by the River." *Progressive Architecture* (July, 1969)

Consultant Contributors

The following professionals have made significant contributions to the work of Richard Dattner & Partners Architects.

Architects
Cowley Prudon LLP
Davis Brody Bond LLP
Gruzen Samton & Partners
Margaret Helfand
Michael Kwartler & Associates
Henri LeGendre
LIRO/Kassner
James McCullar & Associates
Schenkel, Schultz
Wechsler, Grasso, Menziuso
Steven Winter Associates
Zaskorski/Notaro

Engineers
Cameron Engineering, P.C.
Daniel Frankfurt P.C.
E.W. Finley
Feld, Kaminetzky & Cohen
Geiger Berger Engineers
Gilsanz Murray Steficek, LLP
Goldreich Page & Thropp
Leslie E. Robertson Associates, R.L.L.P.
Parsons Brinckerhoff Quade & Douglas
Robert Silman Associates, P.C.
Rodney D. Gibble Consulting Engineers
Rosenwasser Grossman Associates
Severud Associates
Stanley Goldstein, PC
Stone & Webster
Ysrael A. Seinuk P.C.

MEP Engineers
Abraham Joselow P.E., PC
Archtech Electrical Corp.
C.T. Vogel, P.E. Consulting Engineer
Caretsky & Associates, Inc.
Chu & Gassman
Cosentini Associates
DVL Consulting Engineers
Flack and Kurtz Consulting Engineers
George Langer Associates
Hartmann & Concessi, P.C
Herbert Kundstadt Associates
I. M. Robbins P.C. Consulting Engineers
Jack Green Associates
Jaros Baum and Bolles
Yuri Katz Associates
Joseph Loring and Associates
KFA Consulting Engineers
Lakhani & Jordan Engineers, PC
Lizardos Associates P.C.
Lockwood Kessler & Bartlett
Mariano D. Molina PC
Peninsula Engineering, Inc
Robert Derector Consulting Engineers
Robert Ettinger Associates
Syska & Hennessy, Inc., Engineers
T/S Associates
Wesler & Cohen Consulting Engineers

Landscape Architects
Abel Bainnson Butz
A. E. Bye & Associates
Blumberg & Butter PC
Imbiano Quigley Landscape Architects
Lager Raabe Landscape Architects
Mathews Nielsen P.C.
Miceli Kulik Williams & Associates
Quennell Rothschild Associates
Thomas Balsley
Vreeland & Guerriero

Lighting
Ann Kale Associates
Domingo Gonzalez Associates
Gary Gordon
Imero Fiorentino Associates
Hillmann DiBernardo & Associates Inc.

Acoustics
Cerami Associates
Peter George & Associates

Graphics
Anthony Russell
Apple Designs, Inc.
Design Sign Systems
Donovan & Green
Kolano Design
Lebowitz/Gould Design
Louis Nelson Associates
Pentagram
Service Station
Wade Zimmerman

Civil/Geotechnical/Environmental
A. James deBruin & Sons
Allee King Rosen & Flemming
ATC Environmental Consultants, Inc.
Edwards and Kelcey
ERM – Northeast
Ethan Eldon & Associates
Ivey, Harris & Walls, Inc.
Keane-Coppelmann Eng., PC
Langan Engineering
Mueser Rutledge Engineers
NAC Environmental
Raamot Associates
Shaindel Environmental Consultants., Inc
TTI Environmental Inc.
Wohl & O'Mara

Food Services
Romano Gatland
Post and Grossbard

Cost Estimators
Accu-Cost Construction Consultants, Inc.
Associated Cost Engineers, Inc.
Federman Construction Consultants, Inc.
Gazetten Contracting Inc.
J.C. Estimating, Inc
Nasco Associates
The McGee Company
V. J. Associates
Nissim Zelouf

Other Consultants
Berzak/ Schoen Consultant
BET Consultants
Building Conservation Associates, Inc.
Burchman Terrio Quist
Carole Slater Esq.
Charles Rizzo & Associates
Construction Specifiers LLP
Davidoff & Malito
Design 2147
Development Consulting Services, Inc.
Dr. Richard Olsen
Georges Piette
Israel Berger & Associates
JAM Consultants, Inc.
Jenkins & Huntington Inc.
Joan H. Geismar Ph.D.
John A. Van Deusen Assoc.
K & R Consulting
Law Offices of Hirschen & Singer
Leonard J. Strandberg Assoc.
Lovell & Belcher, Inc.

Nicholas Browse & Associates
Olympus International A.G.
Philip Habib Associates
Reginald D. Hough
Robert Schwartz & Associates
Rosenman & Colin
Saccardi & Schiff
Sandler Security Consulting
Steven Pine Associates
Mark Seiden, Esq.
Tom Schwinn
The RBA Group
Urbitran Associates
VS&R Exhibit Planning & Exhibit Design
Warren Panzer

Interior Design
Susan Ecker
Margery Thomas
Schaefer Cassety Inc
Sheelagh Manno

Athletic/Pool
Counsilman/Hunsaker & Associates

Renderers/Model Makers
Michael Berardesco
A.C. Bergmann
George Raustiala
Richard Tengurian
Svonim Tesla
Todd Architectural Models
David Williams/3D Media
Bernard Zalon

Collaborators

Richard Dattner & Partners Architects PC

Partners
Richard Dattner FAIA
Joseph Coppola AIA
William Stein AIA
Bernard Zipprich AIA
Beth Greenberg AIA

Associates
Robin Auchincloss AIA
Paul Bauer AIA
Michael Daniels AIA
Federico Del Priore AIA
Jeffrey Dugan AIA
Perry Hall AIA
John Lam AIA

Architects
John Woelfling RA
John Ziedonis RA
Cylvia Cruz-Beck
George Cumella
Craig Graber
Adam Koffler
Matthew Kuria
Boris Lakhman AIA
Chihming Lin
Robert Markinson
Beata Matysiak
Julio Morales
Kristin Nelson
Carole Richards
David Sachs
Robert Schwartz
Pete Sprung
Maurice Tobias
Anita Wright

Administrative Staff
Frances Soliven
Fatima Griffith
Desiree Rucker-Addison
Karla Roman
Deidre Salon

Former Contributors
Craig Abel
Jennifer Adler
Margaret Alvarez
James Anderson
Helen Angeles
Robert Axten
Terry Bailey
Niv Ben-Adi
Christopher Berg
Amy Benenson
Frank Bonura
Walter Broner
Claribel Byer
Mark Camera
Felicia Campanella
Mark Campione
Rick Carpenter AIA
Ted Ceraldi
Songsri Chang
Sandra Chase
David Cipperman
Harvey Cohn
Kevin Dakan
Keith Daniels
Gerald Davis
Robert Drake AIA
Merle Deen
Yvonne DelaCruz
Stefanos Eapen
Susan Ecker
Dan Erez
Philippe Erville
Michael Esposito
David Falk
Crystal Felder

Diego Feraru
Mimi Florance
Jenny French
Evelyn Gamez
Elizabeth Geary
Haritini Geiser
Julie Gillis
Mark Ginsberg AIA
Pat Guadagno
Barry Goldsmith
David Hess
Daniel Heuberger
Carolyn Hunter
Jonathan Jaffe
Rowena Kabigting
Barbara Kalish
Michelle Kayon
Jeffry Keiffer
William Kelm
Laura Kiaulenas
Jonathan Klausz
Randy Korman
Carolinn Kuebler
Paritosh Kumar
Betsy Lanier
Naomi Leiseroff
Michael Lenahan
Gloria Lim
Judy Lowenthal
Jeffrey Luy
David Mann
Katrina Maxino
Mike Mayo
Deborah McManus
Deanna C. Medina
Richard Metzner
Henry Meltzer
Evelyn Menendez
Victor Migneco
Daniel Mitchell
Monty Mitchell
Bernardo Ngui
Deborah Norden
Michael Notaro
Jaime Ortega AIA
Mathew Park
Nora Pieter
Anthony Pileggi
Frank Prial Jr.
Aron Portnoy
Hernando Quijano
Ramon Quiray
Channing Redford
John Reistetter
John Roundtree
Lidia Ruiz
Carlos Sainz
Antonette Santos
Steve Secon
Gabriel Seijas
Fariba Shirdel
Kenneth Shook AIA
Ellen Shoskes
Michael Stein
David Stuart
Henrietta Susser
Donna Taraschuk
Margery Thomas
Henry Thompson
Omolade Jacob Tukuru
Solita Wakefield
Linda Walker
Lois Weinthal
Angela Wheeler
Roger Whitehouse
Allan Willig
Susan Woo
Bernard Zalon

Acknowledgments

Photography Credits

John Back: 204 (1); 205 (2,3)

Geoffrey Clements: 104 (1,2); 105 (3,4)

Richard Dattner: 19 (2,3); 20 (1); 21 (3); 42 (1); 43 (2); 44 (4); 51 (4); 52 (1 – art by Susan Davis,2); 53 (3,4); 54 (1); 97 (1); 108 (1); 114 (1); 115 (3,4); 124 (1); 126 (1); 127 (3,4); 129 (4); 154 (1); 155 (2,3); 156 (4); 157 (7); 158–159; 161 (2); 163 (3); 170 (2); 172 (1,2); 173 (4); 177 (3); 178 (1,2); 179 (3); 180–181; 184 (2); 185 (3); 186 (1); 187 (4); 194 (1,2); 197 (3,4); 234 (1); 235 (3); 236 (5,6); 238 (2); 239 (3,4)

D. James Dee: 39 (8,9 – artist Sung-Ho Choi)

Scott Frances/ESTO: 130 (1); 132 (2); 133 (4); 134 (6,7); 135 (8,9)

Jeff Goldberg/ESTO: 24 (1); 36 (1); 38 (5); 39 (6,7); 65 (3); 70 (1); 71 (3,4); 72 (5); 73; 74–75

Stan Greenberg: 179 (4)

IE Engineering: 156 (5,6); 157 (8)

Rosanna Liebman: 47 (2–5); 50 (1,2); 51 (3)

C.E Martin/The New Yorker: 18 (1)

Peter Mauss/ESTO: 65 (2); 84 (1); 85 (3); 86; 88 (5); 89 (6,7); 113 (2,3); 116 (1,2) 117 (4); 118 (5,6); 129 (1); 148 (1); 150 (3,4); 151 (6,7); 152–153; 226 (1); 227 (2); 228–229

Norman McGrath: 17 (1,2); 25 (3); 26 (4,5); 27 (6,7); 28 (8); 29 (9,10); 30 (1); 31; 32 (4,5); 33 (6,7); 65 (1); 76 (1,2); 77; 78 (4,5); 79 (6,7); 80–81; 129 (2,3); 136 (1); 137 (2,3); 138–139; 140 (1); 141 (2,3); 142–143; 144 (1,2); 145 (3); 146 (4); 147 (5); 161 (1,3); 164 (1); 165 (2); 166 (1); 167 (3,4); 168 (1); 169 (2,3)

NYC Police Department: 109 (5)

R Propper: 237 (7,8)

Laura Rosen: 22 (1); 23 (3,4 – mural by Knox Martin); 49 (1); 56 (1,2); 57 (4); 97 (4); 98 (1); 99 (2); 100–101

Pete Sprung: 17 (3); 34 (1); 35 (2); 37 (2); 45 (5,6); 49 (2–4); 55 (2); 60 (1); 61 (2,3); 62 (1,2); 63 (3,4); 65 (4); 113 (4); 125 (2); 161 (4); 162 (1); 163 (2); 188 (1); 192–193; 196 (1,2); 200 (1,2); 201 (3)

Roy Wright: 17 (4); 37 (3); 40 (10), 41 (11); 58 (1,2); 59 (3); 68 (1); 69 (4,5); 190 (1); 191 (2); 198 (1); 199 (2,3)

Rendering & Graphics Credits:

3D Media: 46 (1); 57 (3); 90 (1,2); 91 (3,4); 174–175; 203 (4); 209 (3); 211 (3); 220 (2); 221 (3); 222 (5); 223 (7); 231 (3)

Al Bergmann: 67 (3); 97 (2,3); 102 (1); 103 (3); 106 (1); 107 (3); 110 (1); 120 (1); 184 (1); 187 (5); 216 (3); 217 (4)

George Cumella: 92 (1,2); 182 (1); 183 (3)

Richard Dattner: 6 (1); 8–9; 11 (1); 13 (2); 14 (3); 15 (4); 82 (1); 84 (2); 103 (4); 106 (2); 111 (2); 123 (4); 151 (5); 171 (3,4); 173 (5); 191 (4); 195 (4); 202 (1); 206 (1); 222 (6) 235 (2)

Donovan & Green: 71 (2)

Perkins Eastman: 122 (1); 123 (3)

Service Station: 109 (4)

Svonim Tesla: 66 (1,2)

Index

Bold page numbers refer to featured projects.